TRAINING FOODSERVICE EMPLOYEES

TRAINING FOODSERVICE EMPLOYEES

A Guide to Profitable Training Techniques

Gen LaGreca

VNR VAN NOSTRAND REINHOLD
New York

Copyright © 1988 by Genevieve LaGreca
Library of Congress Catalog Card Number 88-10646
ISBN 0-442-25982-4

Printed in the United States of America

Van Nostrand Reinhold
115 Fifth Avenue
New York, New York 10003

Van Nostrand Reinhold International Company Limited
11 New Fetter Lane
London EC4P 4EE, England

Van Nostrand Reinhold
480 La Trobe Street
Melbourne, Victoria 3000, Australia

Macmillan of Canada
Division of Canada Publishing Corporation
164 Commander Boulevard
Agincourt, Ontario M1S 3C7, Canada

16   15   14   13   12   11   10   9   8   7   6   5   4   3   2   1

Library of Congress Cataloging-in-Publication Data

LaGreca, Gen, 1947-
    Training foodservice employees: a guide to profitable training
techniques   /   Gen LaGreca.
        p.   cm.
    Includes index.
    ISBN 0-442-25982-4
    1. Food service employees—Training of.   I. Title.   II. Title:
Training food service employees.
    TX911.3.T73L34 1988
    647'.95068'3—dc19   88-10646

To Rick

Contents

Preface

The idea for this book came from Phil Mason, then editor for CBI Books. After reading an article I wrote for *Restaurant Business* magazine on training foodservice employees, he suggested I write a book on the subject. After his remark, I began noticing the many inquiries I was getting from foodservice operators such as "Is there a guide that will tell me how to write a personnel handbook?" "Are there some sample training materials available that I can use to help me develop my own programs?" or "How can I find out more about training trainers?" In addition, my seminar, "Tools for Training," conducted for the National Restaurant Association, had been well attended for years by operators throughout the country. Despite great interest in training foodservice employees, there were few publications on the subject.

This book describes methods of training foodservice employees. It includes illustrative material which the reader can readily adapt for use in any operation. The emphasis throughout is on application, as the book guides the operator step-by-step through designing an effective training program.

This book is written for all foodservice operators, whether their concern is fine dining, informal dining, cafeteria service, or fast food. It is written for back-of-the-house as well as front-of-the-house managers. Many of my examples come from the dining room, since this is the area for which my clients most often request training and where my experience leans most heavily. However, all the methods of training, such as orientating the new employee, writing training manuals, training trainers, evaluating the trainee, and monitoring performance, apply to all types of foodservice operations and all areas within an operation.

I would like to thank Robert Palmer, former legal counsel for the National Restaurant Association, for his advice on some matters pertaining to employment law. I am also grateful to various companies with which I have worked for allowing me to reproduce some of their training materials. Most of these materials were written by me, and I would be truly at a loss to illustrate many points without their inclusion. Specifically, I would like to thank the following companies for permission to include their training materials: Inhilco, Inc., operators of the World Trade Center restaurants in New York; Mr. Steak, Inc., a national chain of family restaurants; and three of the most popular restaurants in Denver, Simms Landing, Marina Landing, and H. Brinker's. I would also like to thank *Restaurant Business* magazine for allowing me to reprint part of the script of its video training tape, "The Professional Server: How to Increase Sales and Tips." In addition, producer Doug Hanes of Transtar Productions assisted with Chapter 9 on using audiovisuals.

Although I have trained thousands of managers and servers on alcohol awareness through conducting the Colorado-Wyoming Restaurant Association's program on this subject, I have excluded treatment of liquor liability in this book because of the numerous programs and materials available from state restaurant associations, the National Restaurant Association, and liquor suppliers.

I encourage all the foodservice operators who read this book to implement its techniques for developing an effective training program and producing an enthusiastic and competent staff.

TRAINING FOODSERVICE EMPLOYEES

PART ONE

INTRODUCTION

1

Is Training Necessary?

Before we discuss how to train employees, I would like to address a more fundamental issue: Is training necessary? Training requires an ongoing commitment of time, effort, and money. Can we justify such a commitment and show that training is really worthwhile?

According to the dictionary, to train means "to guide the development of; to instruct so as to make proficient or qualified." Is it necessary to instruct and guide your employees, or should they be able to learn the job on their own? After all, your employees are adults (or almost adults, in many cases). Because they seek employment, should they not make it their business to learn the job that offers gainful employment, without any special effort on your part?

The following is an example of an actual incident that we can use as a lesson. I was working for a restaurant when a young woman was hired as the new coat-checker. She was told to report to work at the start of the dinner shift. Since the hostess station was located next to the checkroom, the hostess was asked to show the new employee how to check the coats of arriving guests. It sounded logical enough. However, the restaurant quickly became busy, and the hostess's attention turned to seating guests. On her first day of work, the new coat-checker found herself left alone. During the course of the evening, she checked a $20,000 mink coat. She was new. She was confused. It was busy. She left the coatroom unattended for a brief period. The coat was stolen.

It was that restaurant's policy to lock furs in the manager's office, as was often done with the particular coat in question, which was a treasured garment of a steady customer. But no one told the new employee of the policy. In fact, no one mentioned security at all. Being so preoccupied with the details of a new job, the new coat-checker accepted the fur without awareness of its value. She was too busy concentrating on what to do with Mr. Smith's hat, and where to place Mr. Jones's umbrella, and how to retrieve #52's overcoat and scarf.

Needless to say, her confidence was shattered as a result of the incident. She cried openly. She wanted to find a hole and bury herself in it. Not a good way to start a new job. The manager had to endure the fury of the owner when he phoned him at home that evening, on his day off, to relate the incident. The customer, although kind and understanding, suffered the loss of a precious belonging at what certainly appeared to be the restaurant's carelessness and she expected full compensation. Everyone was miserable except the thief who, incidentally, was never caught.

How could this incident have been avoided? How could the restaurant have insured that important information was communicated to the new coat-checker? Any one or combination of the following measures may have prevented the error made by the new employee, at little or no expense to the restaurant.

1. Having the new employee come in one hour before the start of her shift, allowing the hostess and/or manager time to explain the job in greater detail.

2. Having the new employee trail an experienced person. All too often, the person formerly doing the job is no longer with the restaurant and is unavailable to train the replacement. If the restaurant had no other coat-checker, another employee who knew the job, such as the hostess, could have been asked to work the checkroom for an evening to train the new person, and the novice would not have been left on her own.

3. Providing the hostess with a checklist of the duties and tasks of the coat-checker. If the hostess were instructed to cover every item on a written list with the new coat-checker and among the listings were the "policy on furs and other valuables," the hostess would have been less likely to have omitted this important information.

4. Giving the new coat-checker a job description. When a trainee is given information in writing about the job, he or she is able to take more initiative in the training. If the new coat-checker had seen a job description that indicated one responsibility as the "safe handling of furs," it may have prompted her to pause and ask for instructions when confronted with the fur.

5. Giving the new employee a training manual. In this case, the coat-checker could have read for herself that furs are locked in the manager's office and acted accordingly.

6. Starting the new person on a slow night. While a certain amount of business is often desirable during training to allow the trainer to cover a variety of circumstances and to allow the trainee sufficient repetitions of the new tasks, it is not usually a good idea to start the new person on a busy night. There simply is not enough time for the novice to ask questions of the trainer or for the trainer to pay much attention to the trainee. Also, the fast pace can evoke stress and anxiety in the person not yet prepared to deal with high volume.

Much of this is obvious and requires a modicum of common sense, rather than a degree in education, to grasp. Why, then, did the coat-checker not receive better training? Was the manager stupid? No, he was intelligent and conscientious. Was the hostess uncaring? No, she was a valuable worker. The problem was that both manager and hostess viewed the coat-checker's job as self-evident, immediately understandable, and not requiring further explanation. After all, you just hang up the coat and give the customer a ticket. What could be simpler? How could it take more than ten minutes to explain the job to someone?

The error, a common one, lies in taking for granted one's own knowlege and skills. Once we have mastered a task, it is easy to lose awareness of the time, often years, that we have spent learning and practicing the task. Once we know how to do something, the task seems so simple that it is difficult to remember what it was like not knowing the task. It is often in this state of mind that we undertake to train a new employee, unaware of his or her mind's requirements to grasp the job.

The need for training lies in the fact that knowledge and skills are not automatic. The very opposite is true. Human beings are born, as Aristotle described it, *"tabula rasa";* the mind is a "blank slate" at birth. Everything we know today, we have learned at some point. In the crib, it is impossible to know that one should not place furs in a restaurant's checkroom. That knowledge has to be acquired.

Every job, even the simplest, has certain details and requirements that are not self-evident to the novice, but must indeed be learned. As an exercise in breaking down what may appear to be self-evident, as all good instructors must do, consider the job of coat-checker in a restaurant. What are some of the tasks one would have to master in order to perform this job properly?

1. General policies and procedures. Uniform and grooming requirements, conduct while on duty, work schedule, meal breaks, etc.

2. Guest relations. Greeting the guest upon arrival, and thanking the guest upon leaving. Helping guests on and off with coats. Answering questions the guest may ask, such as where restrooms, cigarette machines, and phones are located.

3. The restaurant's system for checking coats. Placing tickets on the coats and giving duplicate tickets to the guests. The maximum number of coats that may be hung on one hanger. Preventing coats from wrinkling.

4. Handling hats, scarves, gloves, umbrellas, briefcases, and packages. The proper handling of these items to avoid their loss. Preventing umbrellas from getting the coats wet.

5. Policy regarding money. Collecting a charge, if any, for checking the coat. Policy on accepting and reporting tips.

6. Security of the coatroom. The handling of furs and other valuables. The importance of attending the checkroom at all times. What to do if one has to leave the checkroom for a brief period.

7. Opening and closing procedures. Dusting, vacuuming, and tidying up the checkroom. How and when these tasks should be done.

When you consider the number of details required to perform this relatively simple job, the answer to our initial question becomes obvious. Yes, it is necessary to instruct the employees, to guide their development. There are simply too many details to know, too many things that can go wrong, and too much at stake for you.

If employees are not provided with the details of their jobs, a very dangerous thing happens: They begin to fill in the missing details. So we see inexperienced persons setting the terms on how their jobs are to be performed. The employees have to do this, since they are expected to perform the jobs. For example, if you do not instruct the new cook on how much cheese to put into the cheese omelet, he will put in his own amount, which may be more than you want. And if you do not specify to the new cleaner how thoroughly you want the shake machine cleaned, he will clean it his own way, which may fall shy of your standards as well as the health inspector's.

After a certain number of repetitions, the employee contracts a case of bad habits. And habits are tenacious. It is far easier to have trained an employee properly at the outset than it is to allow a bad habit to form and later try to correct it. Tally the untold costs of the bad habits of your employees, which chew up your bottom line in countless ways. The incorrect portioning, the waste, the unsatisfied guests, the sales that were never made, the wear and tear on equipment, the breakage, and more—how much could have been avoided through meticulous and thorough training programs that instilled good work habits?

Some employers contend that hiring experienced people is the way to circumvent training. An experienced coat-checker, for example, would not be very likely to lose a fur coat. That may be true, and experience may often be helpful in reducing training time and costs. But, caution! Experienced people still need familiarity with your particular menu, service standards, and other policies. Also, experienced people may bring bad habits with them, or simply do things differently than you would like to see them done. For example, I know very experienced waiters who open a bottle of wine by unabashedly placing the bottle between their legs and pulling out the cork. I know a bartender who, after 30 years of experience, continues to shake his entire body, instead of merely his wrists, each time he mixes a drink. So much for experience—it is a double-edged sword. Training is needed for experienced people as well as novices.

It is also pyschologically damaging when new employees fail to receive proper training. Part of the turnover that plagues our industry actually occurs during an employee's first 30 working days. This turnover is often the result of insufficient training. It is perfectly understandable that lack of training would lead to a person's quitting or being fired.

People beginning a new job are often confused and anxious. They may worry about whether they will succeed at the job. They urgently need knowledge and skills so that they can function. If the needed information is given to them in a calm and organized manner (insofar as this is possible in a busy restaurant), learning the job can be relatively easy and enjoyable. They can become efficient and confident. However, if they do not get the information they need in order to know what they are doing, they become further lost and confused. There may be enormous demands—to operate a cash register, to balance dishes on a tray, to deal with waiting customers, to interact with the staff. The problem is that employees who do not know how to deal with these demands can come under stress. They may then become disgruntled, resenting the manager, the operation, and even the customers. They may either quit or behave so badly that they get fired. This is how the lack of training contributes to turnover. And the cost of turnover further erodes the bottom line.

Training produces confident and competent employees. Training instills good work habits. Training has a profound effect on employees' performance and on an operation's profitability. The institution of systematic and comprehensive training programs is not a luxury, but a necessity for a restaurant in today's competitive market.

Factors Affecting Job Performance

While training is necessary to insure proper performance by employees, it alone is not sufficient to solve all your performance problems. Other factors are also necessary. They include selection, motivation, and operational environment.

Selection

Employees must be suited for the job and capable of being trained. For example, if you hire a very shy and introverted young man, it may not be possible to train him to become an outgoing, bubbly, exuberant waiter. The best skills training program in the world cannot make fundamental changes in a person. Someone whose strengths and interests do not lie in customer relations may not be trainable as a waiter.

Motivation

It is not enough that employees *know* how to perform, they must also *want* to perform. They may be trained by the best methods possible, but if they are unmotivated, you will not get the desired performance.

There are many reasons why an employee may not be motivated. For example, lack of motivation could stem from job conditions, over which the manager can exert a strong influence. The employee may feel underpaid or overworked, or may resent being criticized by the manager in front of others, to name a few possibilities. Lack of motivation could also stem from personal problems, over which the manager may exert little or no influence. The employee may feel guilty for not finishing school and pursuing a different career; or the person may be preoccupied with marital or other problems to the extent that he or she cannot concentrate on the work. In cases in which the employee knows how to perform but fails to do so, lack of motivation may be the problem. The manager can often, though not always, influence an employee's motivation.

Operational Environment

The employee may have been selected properly, trained thoroughly, and be strongly motivated, but still be unable to perform well due to operational problems. The employee may not have the tools or the time to perform well. For example, a waitress may be told to suggest soup to the guests as an appetizer. She may know how to suggest soup and may be motivated to suggest soup, convinced that the additional sales will help tips. However, this server probably will not suggest soup if there is a shortage of soup spoons or bowls and she will have to waste time with each soup order searching for supplies. Well-trained, motivated employees also need favorable operating conditions to perform their jobs properly.

This book is concerned with training: with establishing a system for training and implementing it in your restaurant. While training is indispensable, I caution you that training alone may not solve all your performance problems. Consideration also needs to be given to the other factors that affect performance.

However, training can have a profound influence on the other factors. For example, assume you hire someone who is not ideally suited for restaurant work. Perhaps the person works slowly and will have difficulty operating at the fast pace necessary during high-volume periods. Through a training program that aims at building speed, the employee may be able to overcome a natural inclination to do things at a slower pace. The person may develop the required speed through training.

Also, training can enhance a person's motivation. By taking the time and effort to train your new employees, you are demonstrating that both they and their work are important to you. By explaining things in a stepwise, organized fashion, you are showing awareness and respect for their intellect; you express your understanding of their mental requirements for learning the job. Training implies respect for the employees, for their minds, and for their work. Most people will respond to this kind of treatment by holding you in esteem and by trying their best to perform well. This is how mutual respect is built.

Lastly, training can improve the operational environment. Referring to our example of the server who will not suggest soup because there is a shortage of soup spoons and bowls, consider how training can improve these operational problems. If employees were trained to carefully empty buspans so that silverware was not accidentally discarded, there would likely be more utensils on hand and hence more soup spoons. If the dishwashers were instructed to promptly return items to the shelves after they were washed, this would likely aid the server in finding soup bowls in stock. Training can improve operational conditions in many ways.

Now that we see the importance of training, our attention will be devoted to finding out how best to train employees in a foodservice operation. Our concern will be with training hourly employees and it will occupy us for the rest of this book. At the end of the book, you will find an exercise on developing a training program for your operation. By the time you reach it, you will be prepared to work through its parts and create a program that is suitable to your restaurant.

Summary

Is it necessary to train employees, or should they be able to learn the job on their own? Training is necessary, since we are all born knowing nothing and every job has certain details and requirements that must be learned. Too much information is required to allow employees to pick things up on their own; too many things can go wrong, with profoundly harmful effects on your business. If employees are not instructed on all aspects of their jobs, they begin to fill in the missing details for themselves. This is how bad work habits are created.

Training is required even if you hire experienced people. Knowledge of your particular menu, service procedures, and other policies must be learned. Also, experienced people may have bad habits that did not bother former employers, but that you will want to correct.

It is also psychologically damaging to employees if they are not properly trained. Demands are made on the employees to perform tasks that they are not prepared to do properly. This causes stress and anxiety, and leads the employees to resent the job, the manager, and the customers. Through this process, failure to train leads to turnover, which in turn leads to higher operating costs.

Training is not the only factor that affects an employee's performance. Careful selection, continued motivation, and a good operational environment are also essential. Training will not only impart knowledge and skills to employees, but it will have a favorable effect on the other factors that influence performance.

This book will focus on the methods to use for training hourly employees in a foodservice operation. The book will end with an exercise which, when completed, will enable you to establish a suitable training program for your operation.

2

Developing a Systematic Approach to Training

A common approach to training foodservice employees is known as the buddy method. It goes something like this: "Hey, Mary, come here for a minute. Meet Jane. She's the new waitress. I'd like you to show her around for a few days and teach her the ropes." This method of training uses an experienced employee, usually one doing the same job, to teach job skills to the new employee. The training is done on the job, with the new person trailing the experienced employee for a day or more. In our example, Jane, the new waitress, will be trained for her job by trailing Mary, the experienced waitress.

The buddy method has some notable virtues:

1. It uses peers as trainers. Hourly employees who do the job regularly may be more familiar with the job's details and more agile at the job than the manager. Also, peers can be less intimidating to the trainee than management-level trainers.

2. It is on-the-job training. When teaching someone a skill, it is essential that the trainee be exposed to the actual work setting: to the tasks, equipment, and procedures that comprise the job.

3. It employs a role model. The trainer serves as a role model. The new employee has an opportunity to see an experienced person perform the job and to emulate that person.

4. It is practical. It is convenient and economical to utilize an hourly employee who is already performing the job as trainer. You probably do not have the time to go into every detail of a new job with each trainee. Therefore the buddy is an essential part of an effective training program.

These benefits will not automatically occur whenever the buddy method is used. In order to be effective, the buddy method must be carefully planned and supervised. There are often serious shortcomings with the buddy method because it is frequently used without being effectively managed. These shortcomings include the following:

1. Instruction can be incorrect. The buddy may not be performing the job according to standards, in which case the buddy is an unsuitable role model. This is how bad habits are passed on. For example, the buddy may be in the habit of smoking cigarettes in a no-smoking area. The trainee will see this behavior and follow suit. Or, the buddy may be a server who does not suggestively sell items to guests. The trainee will then learn to take the guests' orders without suggesting items to boost sales. The buddy method will not work unless the buddy is doing the job correctly.

2. Instruction can be incomplete. Unless properly trained for the role of instructor and supported by written training guidelines, the buddy will be likely to omit important information. Even the simplest jobs involve many details, and the buddy cannot be expected to remember them all while instructing the trainee. For example, the buddy may explain some of the steps in using the deep fat fryer, but omit others. So, the trainee may know that he needs to set the fryer to a certain temperature, but he may not know when to turn the fryer on. He could come in at 9 A.M. and unthinkingly turn the fryer on, even though he would not be using it until 11:30 A.M., which would be costly and unnecessary. Without preparation for the role as instructor and support materials for guidance, the buddy could very easily fail to communicate important information. There is another reason why training is often incomplete. The buddy is working while teaching. When the restaurant gets busy, the training is likely to be forgotten and all attention focused on getting orders out, waiting on customers, clearing tables, and so on. In our earlier example of the hostess training a new coat-checker, the hostess became busy seating customers, and as a result neglected to instruct the new employee on the restaurant's policy for handling furs.

3. Bad attitudes can be passed on. If the buddy has a negative attitude about the establishment, it can easily be passed on to the new employee. For example, whether justified or not, the buddy may feel that you have taken advantage of him. He may warn the new employee never to do you a favor,

like working on his scheduled day off or doing tasks that are not part of his regular job, because you will then call upon him for these favors all the time. If you do not carefully choose the buddy, someone with a bad attitude can affect the attitude of the trainee.

4. Poor teaching skills can inhibit learning. The buddy may be competent at doing the job, but may not be good at teaching the job to someone else. In sports, for example, not every good tennis player makes a good teacher of the sport. The buddy may lack the patience to repeat things or to do tasks in a slow and stepwise manner so the newcomer can grasp them. The buddy may not be articulate in explaining what he or she is doing or may not take the time to allow the trainee to practice. If you choose the buddy for competence at performing the job, but you do not consider the buddy's communication and teaching skills, the results can be very disappointing.

5. There may be no provision to test the trainee. All too often there is no formal means of evaluating the trainee. After spending a few days with the new person, the buddy may feel the trainee is grasping the job. On this basis alone, you may end the training period and put the trainee on his or her own. Of course, the trainee knows a number of things after trailing the buddy for a few days. However, a good deal of information and skill may still be lacking. If you do not have any formal means of evaluating the trainee, you have no assurance that the training has been effective.

For all the above reasons, you need to carefully plan and implement a *system* for training. The buddy method can be an indispensable part of an effective training program, but only if it is properly implemented and managed. If you randomly select the buddy from the available warm-body pool on duty at the moment you need a trainer, you do not have a training system at all—you are leaving training to chance, and chances are the results will not be good.

In order to develop an effective system for training, you need to address and answer the following questions:

1. What needs to be taught? You need to clearly define exactly how you want each job performed before you can teach someone else the job. This involves breaking each job into tasks and breaking each task into steps. For example, in order to train a counter person in a fast-food restaurant, you would first need to break this job down into tasks. These tasks might include the following: how to greet the customer and take the order, how to call the order in, how to ring up the sale, and how to accept the customer's payment and make change. Each of the tasks would then need to be broken down into steps. When this is done, you will have a clear idea of precisely how you want

each task performed. This process of job analysis, which we will discuss in detail in later chapters, is necessary before you can teach someone a skill.

2. Who needs training? Obviously, new employees need training, since they are unfamiliar with your operation. It is more difficult to determine if veteran employees need training, because their poor performance may be the result of lack of training, inappropriate selection, poor motivation, or operational problems, as mentioned previously. A good rule of thumb is that if you have seen an employee perform a task correctly at least twice (once could always be an accident) then chances are the employee's failure to correctly perform that same task on other occasions is not due to lack of knowledge and skills, and additional training will fail to correct the problem. (The employees may need regular reminders of what is important to you, but they will not need training.)

3. Who will do the training? How will you select, develop, and motivate the trainers?

4. How will the training be done? How will the trainer teach the trainee the necessary skills? What materials will be developed to aid the trainer and trainee?

5. How will you know if the training has been successful? What method will you use to evaluate trainees, to see if they have acquired the knowledge and skills necessary to perform the job?

6. How will you maintain performance standards after the training program is completed? What will you do in order to insure that newly trained employees will continue to perform according to the standards they have been taught? How will you avoid the slackening off in performance so often seen after the training period is completed and the new employees are left on their own?

7. What are the costs and benefits of training? Until you have proven to yourself that the benefits far outweigh the costs of training, you will not be wholeheartedly motivated to develop and implement a training program. Training takes time and effort, especially when you are developing the programs. You will need to be fully prepared for the costs of training and convinced of the benefits to you in order to sustain your motivation. Training requires a commitment.

These questions require careful consideration, and key decisions need to be made. When this planning process is completed, you will have developed a system for training your employees.

Here is an example of how the managers of one restaurant addressed the key questions and developed their training system:

1. What needs to be taught? They decided that a general orientation to the restaurant had to be given and job skills needed to be taught. They developed an orientation handbook and two training manuals. One manual had three sections, for bussers, servers and hosts (the three front-of-the-house positions), and another manual had four sections, for prep cooks, fry cooks, broiler cooks, and dishwashers (the four back-of-the-house positions).

2. Who needs training? New employees needed to be trained, and for this purpose they developed a comprehensive training program. Veteran employees also needed retraining in certain areas. They implemented a system of monthly communication meetings for the current staff to address areas where retraining was needed.

3. Who will do the training? They selected and developed trainers. They rewarded their trainers by paying them a higher wage during the time spent training new employees.

4. How will the training be done? A trainer held meetings with new employees after the shift. These meetings would last one hour every day for the first two weeks of employment. The trainer used a checklist of tasks to keep a record of what needed to be taught, what had already been taught, and what remained. Both trainer and trainee referred to the training manual during the lessons. The trainee also trailed a trainer for a few days before obtaining his or her own station.

5. How will you know if the training has been successful? Each trainee was asked to take a written exam to demonstrate knowledge of the job. The trainee was also appraised using a performance evaluation specially designed for his or her job position.

6. How will you maintain performance standards after the training period is completed? The employee's performance was periodically rated using the performance evaluation form. Managers reviewed performance with employees and set goals in areas where corrective action was needed. The managers would follow-up to assure that problems were corrected.

7. What are the costs and benefits of training? There were initial costs of preparing the orientation materials, training checklists, manuals, quizzes, and performance evaluation forms. The ongoing costs included the trainers' and trainees' salaries while they worked on the job and had training meetings during the first two weeks of employment. The meetings amounted to a total

of approximately 20 hours off the job. In addition, there were the payroll costs of one-hour meetings once a month for the staff. The benefits were considered far more substantial than the costs because of all of the ways in which performance is affected by training.

This is just one example of how foodservice operators designed a training program that worked for them. Other approaches are also possible, and we will be discussing some of them.

The rest of this book is devoted to addressing the key issues of concern in developing a system for training and to arriving at the answers best suited for your operation. The goal of the book is to guide you in developing a system so that you are controlling training rather than leaving it to chance. The development of a carefully planned system will produce dividends that will reflect in improved employee performance and greater guest satisfaction.

SUMMARY

A common approach to training in the foodservice industry is known as the buddy method. Using this approach, the new employee trails an experienced person on the job, observing and practicing the job under the experienced worker's supervision. This method has the following virtues: It uses peers as trainers, it is on-the-job training, it employs a role model, and it is practical. However, if the buddy method is not carefully planned and managed, it often leads to the following problems: Instruction is incorrect, instruction is incomplete, bad attitudes of the trainer are passed on to the trainee, poor teaching skills inhibit learning, and no provision is made to test the trainee.

In order to develop an effective system for training, you need to go beyond the random selection of buddies to addressing and answering the following questions: What needs to be taught? Who needs training? Who will do the training? How will the training be done? How will you know if the training has been successful? How will you maintain performance standards after the training program is completed? What are the costs and benefits of training?

The rest of the book will address the above key issues of concern and guide you in developing training systems that are practical for your operation.

PART TWO

ORIENTATION

3

How to Introduce the New Employee to the Job

In the next three chapters, we will be concerned with answering the question, "What do you need to teach?" The subject matter divides into two categories: orientation and skills. The new employee needs a general familiarization with the operation as well as training in the specific skills required to perform the job. Orientation will be addressed in this chapter and skills training in the two chapters that follow. Orientation training is not at all as complex as skills training. It should be done prior to beginning skills training. Also, one gets a great deal of mileage from an orientation program, because it can be used to train all new hourly employees, regardless of their position within the operation.

Orientation is the act of familiarizing new employees with the physical layout, informing them of the general policies and procedures of the establishment, and introducing them to their co-workers. The purpose of orientating new employees is twofold: to impart knowledge and to motivate.

New employees urgently need knowledge in order to function. Your orientation gives them the basic information they need to begin to feel comfortable in your establishment and to know what is expected of them.

Orientation also enhances employees' motivation. They are more likely to form a positive impression of you and your establishment if you are organized and thorough in your orientation. They will feel you are competent and respect you for it. They will also form the conclusion that the rules are important, by virtue of your having carefully explained them. In addition, they will feel that you value them as employees if you have taken the time to acclimate them to their new surroundings. Every new employee gets all these nonverbal messages from you implicitly, simply by your orientation training: that you are well organized, that the establishment's rules are important, and that he or she is valued as an employee. Most people will likely respond to this approach with respect for you and for their jobs. This is how orientation affects the new employee's motivation.

How do you handle orientation? An effective orientation program can be developed that consists of three components: the orientation checklist, the personnel handbook, and the follow-up meetings. Let us examine each component in detail.

The Orientation Checklist

The orientation checklist is an enumeration of all the items you wish to explain to the new employee. There are usually 20 or more different points you need to make and it is difficult, if not impossible, to retain all of this information in your head. A written checklist is a guide to help you remember all the important points you want to cover with the new employee. A checklist assures completeness and consistency in orientating all employees.

You should explain each point on the checklist to the new employee. In a small operation, the general manager or owner should do the orientation training. In a larger operation, the department manager should orientate the new employee. While many aspects of training must be delegated to subordinates, I do not recommend that orientation be delegated. This is your chance to develop a relationship with the new employee. In many operations the manager may not often speak directly to the employee, so orientation becomes one of the rare chances for manager and new employee to get to know each other. Also, orientation is your opportunity to communicate your philosophy and overall standards to the new employee. This message is much more forceful if it comes from you. For example, I remember starting a waitress job while attending school. On my first day, the owner of the restaurant told me that he would try to accommodate guests in whatever they requested. He told me that even if a guest asked for spaghetti and meatballs (which was not on the menu of this seafood restaurant) I should check with the manager to see whether we could make it before telling the guest we did not have it. I always remembered this policy, and I do not think it would have impressed me nearly as much if an hourly employee, the buddy, had said it. So, whenever possible, the manager should conduct orientation.

Orientation should include those policies and procedures that are applicable to all or many employees, such as pay procedures, parking for employees, meal policies, and safety rules. It is not job skills training, so it should avoid including detailed information about any one particular job, such as the portioning of roast beef in a sandwich. Orientation can communicate to the employee that proper portioning and control of waste are important, whereas job skills training will tell the employee specifically how to control waste on the job. Refer to Figure 3-1, the orientation checklist, for a suggestion of points to cover during orientation.

Figure 3-1. Orientation checklist. (Courtesy of Hospitality Industry Training, Inc.)

NAME _____ DATE HIRED _____

INTRODUCTION TO THE COMPANY

_____ WELCOME—Happy to have you aboard. Your position is _____. supervisor is _____. We are an Equal Opportunity Employer. Your employment status is full time/part time.

_____ HISTORY AND ORGANIZATION OF CO.—How we began, our restaurant concept, menu(s), style of service, customers, hours of operation, owners, managers, organization chart.

_____ PHILOSOPHY—Courtesy toward guests, pleasing the guest is our goal, we stand for quality, mutual respect in dealing with each other, handling problems—we encourage you to speak to management (our open-door policy).

BENEFITS

_____ Vacations.
_____ Sick time.
_____ Insurance—medical, dental, life, eligibility, how to enroll.
_____ Worker's Compensation.
_____ Training—our training programs, becoming certified in a position.
_____ Promotion from within.
_____ Award/bonus programs—employee of the month, sales incentives, etc.
_____ Meals—free or discounted, what may be eaten, when and where to take meal breaks, what may not be eaten or drunk, policy on eating/drinking on shift.

POLICIES

_____ APPEARANCE/DRESS CODE

_____ Hygiene, grooming.
_____ Uniforms—receipt and return of, laundering, replacing worn uniforms, items you must furnish at your own expense.

Figure 3-1. *(continued)*

_____ Shoes—type required, policy on sandals and sneakers.
_____ Name tag.
_____ Hair—length, pulled back, facial hair on men.
_____ Hands/Nails—scrubbed, manicured, policy on polish.
_____ Jewelry and cosmetics.

_____ CONDUCT

_____ Attendance, punctuality, doctor's note for repeated absences.
_____ Behavior in front of guests.
_____ Use of obscene language and other disrespectful behavior is not allowed.

_____ ATTITUDE

_____ Attitude toward guests—courtesy, pleasure to serve them, appreciation for their visits.
_____ Attitude toward your job—take it seriously, be conscientious and thorough.
_____ Attitude toward co-workers and management—courtesy, respect, willingness to help.

_____ JOB PERFORMANCE

_____ Job description or checklist. Job duties.
_____ Work schedule, days off.
_____ Breaks—when scheduled, paid or unpaid, punching in and out.
_____ Probationary period.
_____ Training program—manual, audiovisual programs, quizzes, your trainer, your responsibility in learning your new job.
_____ Performance evaluations.

_____ PAY PROCEDURES

_____ Your wage is $_____ per _____ .
_____ Time cards—punching in and out in uniform, signatures on time cards, not punching anyone else's card.
_____ Policies on overtime, advances, loans.
_____ Payday is _____ and covers the work period beginning _____ and ending _____. You will receive your first paycheck _____.
_____ Policy on wage increases.

_____ PAPERWORK/FORMS

      _____ W-4 form, withholding, dependents.
      _____ Insurance forms.
      _____ Tip declaration form—you are required by law to declare 100% of your tips, procedure for doing so.
      _____ Alcohol awareness statement—it is against the law to serve alcohol to minors or to persons who are already intoxicated.
      _____ Insurance forms.

_____ SAFETY—kitchen safety, fire safety systems, preventing accidents, slippery floors, disconnecting equipment prior to cleaning, handling knives/equipment, lifting heavy trays, reporting accidents/illnesses, emergency procedures.

_____ SANITATION—washing hands, keeping hands off food and eating surfaces of dishes, glasses and utensils, cleaning your work station, reporting all pest sightings to management, safe temperatures for keeping food, communicable diseases.

_____ MISCELLANEOUS OTHER POLICIES

      _____ Waste control.
      _____ Breakage, errors—your responsibility.
      _____ Nonsmoking areas.
      _____ Employee parking.
      _____ Employee restrooms, use of guest restrooms not permitted.
      _____ Personal phone calls/visits from friends and relatives.
      _____ Use of facilities before or after working hours.
      _____ Reporting change of name, address, phone.
      _____ Lockers.
      _____ Property removal.
      _____ Work permits for minors, proof of age for service of alcoholic beverages, alien registration, etc.

_____ DISCIPLINARY PROCEDURES

      _____ Policy on verbal and written warnings for violation of rules.
      _____ Failure to correct problem can ultimately lead to dismissal.
      _____ Major infractions—can lead to immediate discharge without prior warning. These include, but are not limited to, the following:

      _____ use or possession of alcohol/illegal drugs on employer's premises, being under influence.
      _____ unauthorized removal of property.
      _____ giving away food.
      _____ fighting/insubordination.

Figure 3-1. *(continued)*

_____ possession of a weapon.
_____ discourtesy/rudeness to guests.
_____ punching someone else's time card.

_____ SEPARATION PROCEDURES

_____ How much notice to give if you are leaving your job.
_____ Exit interviews.
_____ Conditions for collecting severance pay.

TOUR AND PERSONAL INTRODUCTIONS

_____ TOUR OF FACILITIES—where schedule and notices are posted/bulletin boards, restrooms, etc.

_____ INTRODUCTIONS—to management, co-workers, trainer.

_____ Do you have any questions?

WELCOME ABOARD! WE'RE VERY HAPPY YOU'RE HERE!

All points on this orientation checklist have been explained to me by my manager, and I feel confident that I understand the policies.

Signature of Employee _____

Signature of Manager _____ Date _____.

It is also a good idea for you and the employee to sign the orientation checklist. This allows you to have a permanent record in the employee's file that he or she has been given certain information. In the event of a discharge and the filing of charges against you by the employee, you will have a document to show to union or government officials that indicates the employee received information on specific policies from you. Also, the signing should have a psychological effect on both of you. It implies that this information is to be taken seriously, and each party, by virtue of signing his or her name, goes on record as having communicated or received the information. People tend to take more seriously a document that they have to sign.

The checklist can be incorporated into a more detailed document, the staff file folder. This folder should be made of heavy card stock and should be the correct size to serve as a personnel file that you can place in your file cabinet. The file folder is a handy way to record a great deal of information, such as the orientation checklist you have reviewed with the employee; other signed statements you wish to keep on file; and the employee's progress through your training programs, wage and position record, attendance record, scores on performance evaluations, and separation information. Refer to Figure 3-2, the staff file folder, for an indication of how all this information can be compactly recorded on one document. This staff file folder has been used by Mr. Steak, Inc., for many years.

The Personnel Handbook

The personnel handbook is a written explanation of the points covered on the checklist. Whereas the checklist is an aid to you in conducting the orientation, the handbook is an aid to the new employee. The reason for both is the same: There is too much information to rely on memory alone to give and receive it. It is impossible for the new employee to remember all the points you cover verbally. Having the material in writing allows the trainee to review the information during free time and not to have to remember everything after being told just once. A handbook will greatly increase the amount of information that is retained by the new employee.

The handbook should be written in simple language. Follow the checklist closely in creating the handbook, but exclude information that changes frequently, such as items on the menu, hours of operation, and the names of key personnel, so the handbook will not become outdated soon after it is issued. It is common to include illustrations to make the handbook easier and more enjoyable to read.

The tone of the handbook should be direct, but not punitive. You want to clearly state your policies, but without scaring the new person before he or she has done anything wrong. For example, "Do not punch anyone else's time card under any circumstances" can be rephrased as "You may only punch your own time card and no one else's." You have essentially said the same thing, but the latter sentence does not have the punitive effect of the former. While you certainly want to communicate your policies, it is not desirable to make new employees feel like they are in prison.

The new employee should be given the handbook upon hiring and should be told to read it before reporting for orientation. In this way, the employee will be familiar with many of your policies prior to your reviewing the orientation checklist together and thus will be better able to retain the

(Text continued on p. 30)

Figure 3-2. Staff file folder. (Courtesy of Mr. Steak, Inc.)

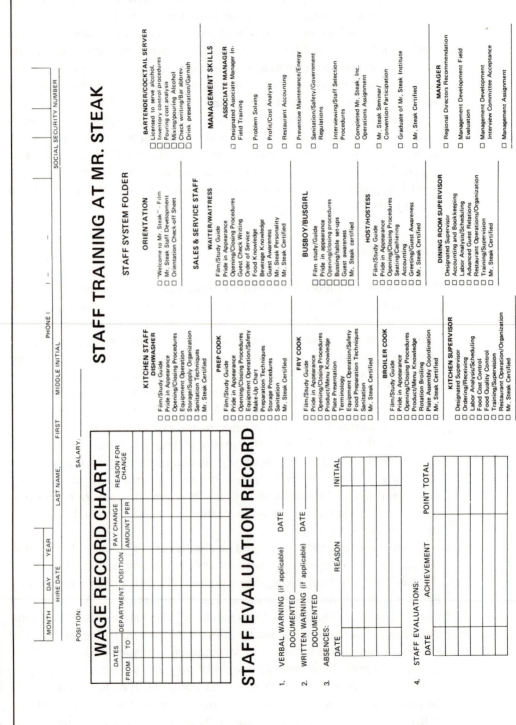

MONTH | DAY | YEAR

HIRE DATE   LAST NAME,   FIRST   MIDDLE INITIAL   PHONE ( )   SOCIAL SECURITY NUMBER - -

POSITION: _____   SALARY: _____

WAGE RECORD CHART

DATES		DEPARTMENT	POSITION	PAY CHANGE		REASON FOR CHANGE
FROM	TO			AMOUNT	PER	

STAFF EVALUATION RECORD

1. VERBAL WARNING (if applicable)   DATE _____
   DOCUMENTED

2. WRITTEN WARNING (if applicable)   DATE _____
   DOCUMENTED

3. ABSENCES:

DATE	REASON	INITIAL

4. STAFF EVALUATIONS:

DATE	ACHIEVEMENT	POINT TOTAL

STAFF TRAINING AT MR. STEAK

STAFF SYSTEM FOLDER

ORIENTATION
- ☐ "Welcome to Mr. Steak". Film
- ☐ Mr. Steak Staff Development
- ☐ Orientation Check-off Sheet

SALES & SERVICE STAFF

WAITER/WAITRESS
- ☐ Film/Study Guide
- ☐ Pride in Appearance
- ☐ Opening/Closing Procedures
- ☐ Guest Check Writing
- ☐ Order of Service
- ☐ Food Knowledge
- ☐ Beverage Knowledge
- ☐ Guest Awareness
- ☐ Mr. Steak Personality
- ☐ Mr. Steak Certified

BUSBOY/BUSGIRL
- ☐ Film study/Guide
- ☐ Pride in appearance
- ☐ Opening/closing procedures
- ☐ Bussing/table set-ups
- ☐ Guest awareness
- ☐ Mr. Steak certified

HOST/HOSTESS
- ☐ Film/Study Guide
- ☐ Pride in Appearance
- ☐ Opening/Closing Procedures
- ☐ Seating/Cashiering
- ☐ Accounting
- ☐ Greeting/Guest Awareness
- ☐ Mr. Steak Certified

KITCHEN STAFF

DISHWASHER
- ☐ Film/Study Guide
- ☐ Pride in Appearance
- ☐ Opening/Closing Procedures
- ☐ Equipment Operation
- ☐ Storage/Supply Organization
- ☐ Sanitation Techniques
- ☐ Mr. Steak Certified

PREP COOK
- ☐ Film/Study Guide
- ☐ Pride in Appearance
- ☐ Opening/Closing Procedures
- ☐ Equipment Operation/Safety
- ☐ Make-Up Chart
- ☐ Preparation Techniques
- ☐ Storage Procedures
- ☐ Sanitation
- ☐ Mr. Steak Certified

FRY COOK
- ☐ Film/Study Guide
- ☐ Pride in Appearance
- ☐ Opening/Closing Procedures
- ☐ Product/Menu Knowledge
- ☐ Plate Presentation
- ☐ Terminology
- ☐ Equipment Operation/Safety
- ☐ Food Preparation Techniques
- ☐ Sanitation
- ☐ Mr. Steak Certified

BROILER COOK
- ☐ Film/Study Guide
- ☐ Pride in Appearance
- ☐ Opening/Closing Procedures
- ☐ Product/Menu Knowledge
- ☐ Rotation Broiling
- ☐ Plate Assembly Coordination
- ☐ Mr. Steak Certified

KITCHEN SUPERVISOR
- ☐ Designated Supervisor
- ☐ Ordering/Receiving
- ☐ Labor Analysis/Scheduling
- ☐ Food Cost Control
- ☐ Food Quality Control
- ☐ Training/Supervision
- ☐ Restaurant Operation/Organization
- ☐ Mr. Steak Certified

BARTENDER/COCKTAIL SERVER
- ☐ Licensed to serve alcohol.
- ☐ Inventory control procedures
- ☐ Pouring cost analysis
- ☐ Mixing/pouring Alcohol
- ☐ Check writing/Bar abbrev.
- ☐ Drink presentation/Garnish

DINING ROOM SUPERVISOR
- ☐ Designated Supervisor
- ☐ Accounting and Bookkeeping
- ☐ Labor Analysis/Scheduling
- ☐ Advanced Guest Relations
- ☐ Restaurant Operations/Organization
- ☐ Training/Supervision
- ☐ Mr. Steak Certified

MANAGEMENT SKILLS

ASSOCIATE MANAGER
- ☐ Designated Associate Manager In-Field Training
- ☐ Problem Solving
- ☐ Profit/Cost Analysis
- ☐ Restaurant Accounting
- ☐ Preventive Maintenance/Energy
- ☐ Sanitation/Safety/Government Regulations
- ☐ Interviewing/Staff Selection Procedures
- ☐ Completed Mr. Steak, Inc. Operations Assignment
- ☐ Mr. Steak Seminar/ Convention Participation
- ☐ Graduate of Mr. Steak Institute
- ☐ Mr. Steak Certified

MANAGER
- ☐ Regional Directors Recommendation
- ☐ Management Development Field Evaluation
- ☐ Management Development Interview Committee Acceptance
- ☐ Management Assignment

TIP AGREEMENT

THE IRS ISSUED REGULATIONS UNDER SUBCHAPTER A OF CHAPTER 61 OF THE INTERNAL REVENUE CODE OF 1954 (26 U.S.C. 6053OO) AFTER CHANGES TO THE APPLICABLE TAX LAW WERE MADE BY SECTION 314 OF THE TAX EQUITY AND FISCAL RESPONSIBILITY ACT OF 1982.

MR. STEAK IS REQUIRED TO ALLOCATE AS TIPS THE EXCESS OF 8% OF THE GROSS RECEIPTS OF THE RESTAURANT FOR A PAYROLL PERIOD (WEEKLY) OVER THE TOTAL AMOUNT OF TIPS REQUIRED TO BE REPORTED BY EMPLOYEES TO THE EMPLOYER FOR THE SAME PAYROLL PERIOD. THE IRS REQUIRES YOU TO REPORT TO MR. STEAK 100% OF THE TIPS YOU RECEIVE BEFORE COMPLETION OF THE WEEKLY PAYROLL.

I, _____, (STAFF MEMBER), UNDERSTAND THAT AS A CONDITION OF MY EMPLOYMENT AT MR. STEAK NO. _____, I AM REQUIRED BY FEDERAL REGULATIONS TO REPORT TO MANAGEMENT 100 PERCENT (100%) OF TIPS RECEIVED BEFORE COMPLETION OF MY WEEKLY PAYROLL.

I UNDERSTAND THAT I WILL BE REQUIRED TO COMPLETE THE TIP CLARIFICATION INFORMATION ON MY WEEKLY TIME CARD. I FURTHER UNDERSTAND THAT FAILURE TO COMPLY WITH THESE PROCEDURES COULD INVOLVE DISCIPLINARY ACTION AND/OR TERMINATION.

SEXUAL HARASSMENT STATEMENT

IT IS THE POLICY OF MR. STEAK, INC. THAT SEXUAL HARASSMENT IN THE WORKPLACE, IN ANY FORM, IS PROHIBITED. SEXUAL HARASSMENT IS DEFINED AS UNWELCOME SEXUAL ADVANCES, OR OTHER VERBAL OR PHYSICAL CONDUCT OF A SEXUAL NATURE WHEN:

1. SUBMISSION TO THE CONDUCT IS EITHER AN EXPLICIT OR IMPLICIT TERM OR CONDITION OF EMPLOYMENT;

2. SUBMISSION TO OR REJECTION OF THE CONDUCT IS USED AS A BASIS FOR ANY EMPLOYMENT-RELATED DECISION AFFECTING THE PERSON WHO REJECTED OR SUBMITTED TO THE CONDUCT, AND;

3. THE CONDUCT HAS THE PURPOSE OR EFFECT OF UNREASONABLY INTERFERING WITH AN AFFECTED PERSON'S WORK PERFORMANCE, OR CREATING AN INTIMIDATION, HOSTILE OR OFFENSIVE WORK ENVIRONMENT.

IT IS ESSENTIAL THAT ALL SUPERVISORS, MANAGERS AND EMPLOYEES ADHERE TO THIS POLICY AT ALL TIMES. FAILURE TO ADHERE TO THIS POLICY WILL RESULT IN APPROPRIATE DISCIPLINARY ACTION. GUIDELINES ISSUED BY THE EQUAL EMPLOYMENT OPPORTUNITY COMMISSION IDENTIFY SEXUAL HARASSMENT AS A VIOLATION OF TITLE – VII OF THE CIVIL RIGHTS ACT OF 1964.

ANY SEXUAL HARASSMENT COMPLAINT SHOULD BE REPORTED TO YOUR MOST IMMEDIATE SUPERVISOR, OR PERSONNEL MANAGER.

FAIR TREATMENT STATEMENT

MR. STEAK STAFF ARE NOT ONLY ALLOWED BUT ARE ENCOURAGED TO AIR ANY PROBLEMS AND COMPLAINTS THEY MAY HAVE IN REGARD TO TREATMENT, CONDITIONS, OR WORK OVER WHICH THE COMPANY MIGHT BE EXPECTED TO HAVE SOME CONTROL.

MR. STEAK'S UNCONDITIONAL POLICY IS THAT EVERY STAFF MEMBER BE TREATED EQUALLY IN MATTERS OF WORKING CONDITIONS, PAY BENEFITS, PROMOTIONS, AND THE RESOLVING OF COMPLAINTS OR PROBLEMS WITHOUT REGARD TO RACE, COLOR, CREED, SEX, AGE OR NATIONAL ORIGIN.

IF YOU HAVE A COMPLAINT, WE WANT TO HEAR FROM YOU. THERE WILL BE NO REPRISAL AGAINST YOU FOR PRESENTING IT. THIS IS HOW YOU GET YOUR COMPLAINT RESOLVED:

1. INFORM YOUR IMMEDIATE SUPERVISOR OF THE COMPLAINT. YOUR SUPERVISOR WILL SOLVE THE PROBLEM IF AT ALL POSSIBLE. HE/SHE WILL LISTEN IN A COURTEOUS MANNER BECAUSE IT IS MANAGEMENT'S DESIRE TO UNDERSTAND AND AID IN SOLVING PROBLEMS WHICH ARISE IN YOUR WORK.

2. WE RECOGNIZE THAT THERE WILL BE TIMES WHEN YOUR SUPERVISOR MAY NOT BE ABLE TO SOLVE YOUR PROBLEM. YOU THEN MAY TAKE YOUR CASE TO THE ASSOCIATE MANAGER. THE MANAGER WILL REVIEW ALL THE FACTS AND SETTLE YOUR PROBLEM IN A FAIR MANNER. IF YOU ARE STILL NOT SATISFIED, YOU MAY THEN GO TO THE MANAGER.

3. IF, AFTER A THOROUGH DISCUSSION OF THE MATTER WITH THE MANAGER, YOU STILL FEEL THE MATTER HAS NOT BEEN RESOLVED TO YOUR SATISFACTION, YOU MAY THEN MAKE AN APPOINTMENT WITH THE DISTRICT DIRECTOR FOR FINAL RESOLUTION.

IT IS MR. STEAK'S POLICY THAT ALL COMPLAINTS AND SUGGESTIONS WILL BE GIVEN FULL ATTENTION AND WILL BE RESOLVED IN THE MUTUAL BEST INTEREST OF THE STAFF MEMBER AND THE COMPANY.

I HAVE READ AND UNDERSTAND THE "TIP AGREEMENT, SEXUAL HARASSMENT AND FAIR TREATMENT STATEMENTS."

DATE: _____

STAFF MEMBER SIGNATURE: _____

MANAGER SIGNATURE: _____

Figure 3-2. *(continued)*

STAFF ORIENTATION CHECKLIST

IN CASE OF **EMERGENCY** WHOM SHALL WE NOTIFY?

NAME: _____ PHONE: _____

ADDRESS: _____ RELATIONSHIP: _____

CHECK OFF BY PLACING DATE IN BOX:

APPLICATION FOR EMPLOYMENT	
FOOD HANDLERS CERTIFICATION	
PAYROLL RELATED POLICY: Overtime, W-4 Signed	
Hourly rate of pay, Payday	
STAFF DISCOUNT: Eligible for Discount.	
SAFETY: Importance of safe work habits, how to	
report injuries/accidents. How to handle	
Emergency situations (injuries/illness, fire)	
PERFORMANCE EVALUATION: Staff disciplinary policy	
STAFF EVALUATION: frequency	
STAFF TRAINING AT MR. STEAK (STAMS)	
Study Guides/Filmstrip	
TOUR THE ENTIRE FACILITY WITH EMPHASIS ON:	
COMMUNICATIONS: Where schedule is posted, how to read it.	
Where all announcements and bulletins are located.	
INTRODUCTIONS: Introduced to other staff members	
and members of management,	
UNIFORM AGREEMENT: Cleaning instructions. Name tag issue	
BENEFIT PROGRAMS: GROUP INSURANCE — Summary of Benefits, Date of Eligibility	
Must sign enrollment or waiver by (date)	
VACATIONS — how earned, when it may be taken.	
HOLIDAYS — Company Holidays.	
OTHER BENEFITS: Review benefit	
summary and give to employee.	
SANITATION: Importance, responsibility to the public.	
STAFF CONCERNS: Who to contact, channels of communication, staff Fair	
Treatment procedure, feedback	
STAFF HANDBOOK — Form signed by staff member indicating handbook has been	
read and understood.	
TARGETED JOB CREDIT QUESTIONNAIRE	
TIME CARDS: How to check in & out, signatures required, time verified	
How to record tips & meals (if applicable)	
PARKING: Do you know where you are allowed to park?	
MISCELLANEOUS: Student verification, minors work permit, Alien registration.	

QUESTIONS: Do you have any other questions about the company, or procedures, or your job as a member of our staff?

ALL TOPICS REFERENCED IN THE STAFF ORIENTATION CHECKLIST CONCERNING MY EMPLOYMENT HAVE BEEN EXPLAINED TO ME AND I UNDERSTAND THEM. I HAVE RECEIVED A COPY OF ALL MATERIAL INDICATED, WHERE APPLICABLE. I UNDERSTAND THAT IF I WANT MORE INFORMATION REGARDING MY EMPLOYMENT WITH MR. STEAK, I MAY CONTACT MY MANAGER OR MY IMMEDIATE SUPERVISOR

_____ _____
STAFF MEMBER'S SIGNATURE   MR. STEAK REPRESENTATIVE

_____ _____
DATE   DATE

SEPARATION REPORT

SEPARATED

MONTH	DAY	YEAR

LAST NAME _____   FIRST _____   MIDDLE INITIAL _____

TYPE OF SEPARATION: Retirement ☐   Resignation ☐   Discharge ☐   Layoff ☐

I. STATED REASON FOR SEPARATION
(Please check the reason that applies)

RESIGNATION

☐ Physical Condition
☐ Family
☐ Returning to School
☐ Secured Better Position
☐ Going into Business for Self

Disliked:
☐ Hours
☐ Supervisor
☐ Type of Work
☐ Wages
☐ Working Conditions
☐ Other Reason: _____

Complete when staff member has RESIGNED:

New Employer _____
Location _____
Nature of new work _____
Pay _____ Hours _____

DISCHARGE

Inadequate:
☐ Ability
☐ Efficiency
☐ Dishonesty
☐ Rules Violation,
   State rule violated: _____
☐ Absenteeism
☐ Tardiness
☐ Will not perform to Mr. Steak standards.
☐ Other Reason: _____

Complete in DISCHARGE cases:

When was staff member notified? _____

How was staff member notified? _____

LAYOFF

☐ Position Abolished
☐ Temporary Work Ended
☐ Reduction of Staff
☐ Other Reason: _____

Complete in LAYOFF cases:

Was staff member offered transfer?   Yes ☐   No ☐
To which department? _____
Why was transfer refused? _____

UNIFORM AGREEMENT

I _____ HAVE RECEIVED _____ UNIFORM(S)
CONSISTING OF _____

VALUED AT $ _____ EACH
FROM MANAGEMENT OF MR. STEAK
NUMBER _____
IDENTIFICATION NUMBER _____

AT MY SEPARATION, I WILL RETURN THE UNIFORM(S) DESCRIBED ABOVE, CLEAN AND PRESSED, OR REIMBURSE MANAGEMENT FOR THE VALUE STATED ABOVE.

I FURTHER UNDERSTAND THAT THESE UNIFORM(S) WILL BE REPLACED FOR REASONS OF NORMAL WEAR AND TEAR, AT NO EXTRA COST, BY THE EXCHANGE OF THE OLD UNIFORM.

STAFF MEMBER _____

MANAGEMENT _____
****

THE ABOVE REMITTANCE OF $ _____
HAS BEEN RECEIVED BY MANAGEMENT.

STAFF MEMBER _____

DATE _____

MANAGEMENT _____

information you present. Also tell the new employee to jot down any questions that come to mind while reading the handbook and to ask them during orientation. The new employee should be asked to review the handbook after you have gone through the checklist together to further reinforce the information. If the employee cannot read English, you may want to ask someone on your staff to explain the handbook.

Both the live orientation and the handbook are necessary if the employee is to retain this information and avoid misunderstandings about your rules.

Refer to Figure 3-3, the personnel handbook, as a guideline for assembling your employee handbook. This handbook is designed for you to fill in the blanks and create your own personalized version. Because laws vary from state to state and change with time, consider this handbook as a guide. The final version of your handbook should be reviewed by an attorney or personnel specialist to be sure it reflects current employment law.

(Text continued on p. 37)

Figure 3-3. Personnel handbook.

TABLE OF CONTENTS

Introduction to the Company

Benefits

Policies

Tour and Personal Introductions

INTRODUCTION TO THE COMPANY

Welcome to _____! We are happy that you have joined our staff.

Equal Opportunity Employer

We are an Equal Opportunity Employer. This means that we will hire, evaluate, and promote solely on the basis of your qualifications and job performance, without regard to race, creed, color, religion, national origin, sex, age, or physical handicap.

History of _____

Our company began in [place and year] and was founded by _____.
[Indicate how the company has developed, the number of units you currently have,

and their locations. You may also want to give the president's or owner's name. Also describe the concept, style of service, and anything you may be noted for, such as fresh seafood, healthy food, prime aged beef, or an on-premises bakery.]

Our Philosophy

Our purpose is to satisfy our guests. That is the goal we all strive for in our work. We expect you to treat our guests like very important people, in the careful way you cook their food, clean the dining room, observe the proper sanitary policies, wash the dishes, or serve the guests. By each person doing his job conscientiously, we show our guests how much we care. A polite, attentive staff leaves a positive impression on guests. So, show our guests it is a pleasure to serve them, tell them that you appreciate their visit, and ask them to come and see us again. If a guest is unsatisfied with something, notify the manager so that he can take corrective action. Our policy is to assure that every guest leaves happy.

It is also our policy to serve quality food to our guests. We expect you to be aware of our high standards when preparing and serving food, and not serve anything to our guests which falls short of these standards.

We think it is important for us to treat each other with respect and consideration. We have an "open-door" policy to management, which means that we want you to let management know of any problems or concerns you may have about your job. We will try to assist you in any way possible.

BENEFITS

You will enjoy many benefits from working for _____. Here are some of them:

[Indicate the benefits you offer, using the orientation checklist section on benefits as a guide. It is recommended that you list benefits before policies in order to motivate the employees. You are first telling them how they will gain from working for you, then you will tell them what is required of them to earn the benefits. Remember that training and opportunities for promotion from within are benefits appreciated by most employees.]

POLICIES

Appearance/Dress Code

Personal Hygiene—A clean, well-groomed appearance makes a positive impression on our guests. So shower daily, use a deodorant, wash your hair often, and use a mouthwash or breath spray.

Figure 3-3. *(continued)*

Your Uniform—[Explain the uniform requirements—slacks, shirts, blouses, dresses, stockings, shoes, name tag, apron, etc. Indicate which items the employee is responsible for furnishing and which will be furnished by management. Indicate policies for laundering or caring for the uniform. Mention that clothes should always be clean and pressed.]

Your Hair—Your hair should be clean and attractively styled. Women with hair at shoulder length or longer need to stylishly restrain it. Men are not allowed to have beards and mustaches must be neatly trimmed. Sideburns are not allowed to extend below the earlobe.

Your Hands and Nails—Hands should be kept clean. Nails should be scrubbed and manicured.

Jewelry and Cosmetics—Jewelry should be limited to a wedding band and a plain watch. Dangling earrings, bracelets, and other ornamental jewelry are not appropriate or safe in the restaurant.

Conduct

We require that you have good attendance and report to work on time. If you are late or absent, others have to do your work as well as their own, and service to our guests suffers. If you are unable to report to work in a rare circumstance, notify your manager as far in advance as possible so that he may find a suitable replacement. Failure to report to work without notifying us is considered inconsiderate and disrespectful, and will be disciplined, as will repeated lateness and absenteeism. If you are absent for three or more days, we require a doctor's note to excuse you.

Your conduct in the restaurant should be professional. This means there should be no obscene language used, and no horseplay in front of the guests. Be courteous and respectful of your guests and co-workers. Rudeness cannot be tolerated in a hospitality business.

Attitude

Having a positive attitude makes it easier for guests, managers, and co-workers to deal with you. Show guests it is a pleasure to serve them by being courteous and helpful. Take your job seriously. By working carefully and conscientiously, you will assure your success. Courtesy also extends to fellow workers and management. Your willingness to assist when needed by doing work other than that which your job requires will be greatly appreciated.

Job Performance

Your supervisor will review your job responsibilities, work schedule, days off, and breaks with you. [Explain policy on schedule—when and where posted, and breaks —when given, how long, and punching in and out.]

Training Program—We will train you for your position. A trainer will be assigned to teach you your job. In addition, you will be asked to read our training manual(s) (and view our audiovisual programs). There will be an examination(s) and performance evaluation to aid us in evaluating your progress. You will get ample opportunity to prepare for the exam(s). We will try in every way to assist you in learning your new job; however, your responsibility will be to make a special effort to grasp the job and ask questions to clarify your understanding of the information presented to you.

Performance Evaluations—A performance evaluation may be requested by you at any time. Your manager will be evaluating your performance every _____ months. These evaluations will give you recognition for your achievements and pinpoint areas in which your work can be improved.

Pay Procedures

Your supervisor will tell you your hourly wage.

You need to tell us when you begin and finish work by punching your time card. This card is our official record of the hours you work, so remember to punch in and out. Punch in when you have your uniform on and are ready to begin your shift. Punch out after you have completed your shift, before you have a meal break or change out of your uniform. You may only punch your own time card and no one else's.

Payday is after _____ P.M. on _____. It covers the work period which begins on _____ and ends on _____.

Overtime must first be approved by a manager.

We are not able to offer advances on pay or loans to employees.

All wage increases are determined by your job performance. Wage increases are not given every time you have a performance evaluation, but rather when management believes they are deserved.

Paperwork and Forms

There are various forms you will need to fill out, and we will be happy to assist you with them. One is the withholding form which the government requires for tax purposes.

If you are a tipped employee, you will also need to sign a form stating that you are aware of your responsibility to report 100% of your tips for tax purposes. [Explain the procedure the employee needs to follow to report tips to you.]

If you serve alcoholic beverages, you will also be asked to sign a statement concerning whom you may not serve.

[Explain any other forms the employee will need to fill out or sign.]

Figure 3-3. *(continued)*

Safety

We ask you to be careful and do your best to prevent accidents. Watch your step on slippery floors. Disconnect equipment prior to cleaning it. When using knives, or equipment with blades, pay attention to what you are doing and do not touch the blades. To prevent back injuries, always lift heavy objects by bending your knees and keeping your back straight.

Report all accidents to your supervisor.

We are protected against fire by fire safety equipment. Your supervisor will explain how to operate this equipment. Know the location of all exits. In the event of an evacuation, proceed in a calm and orderly manner and assist guests in exiting. Follow the instructions of your supervisor.

Sanitation

For the health of our guests, as well as for your own health, always follow the rules of sanitation.

Hands carry germs, so wash them often, and always after visits to the restroom. Remember to keep hands off the eating surfaces of dishes, glasses, cups and utensils.

Clean and dry your work station, so germs will not have a chance to spread. Report all pest sightings to your manager.

Always keep cold foods colder than 40 degrees Fahrenheit and keep hot food hotter than 140 degrees Fahrenheit. Germs spread fastest between 40 and 140 degrees, so we must not allow food to remain at these temperatures.

Of course, you should not work if you have an illness which other people can catch. If you have a communicable disease, you must notify your manager.

Miscellaneous Other Policies

Waste Control—In order be profitable, we much watch our costs very closely. Know the correct portion sizes and avoid overportioning food. By following proper handling and cooking procedures, you can minimize spoilage.

Breakage and Errors—[Explain your policies on breakage and on addition errors on checks. Are employees required to pay for their losses? Indicate that repeated breakage and errors in excess of the acceptable limits is subject to disciplinary warnings.]

Nonsmoking Areas—Employees are not allowed to smoke in front of the guests or in food preparation areas. You may smoke [indicate where and when].

Employee Parking—[If you have an employee parking area, indicate where it is. If not, you may want to advise employees on where to find parking.]

Restrooms—Your supervisor will show you where the employee restrooms are. Employees are not allowed to use the guest restrooms.

Personal Phone Calls and Visits—We ask that you tell your family and friends not to phone or visit you while you are working, except in an emergency.

Use of Facilities—[Describe your policies regarding employees dining or drinking at the restaurant when they are not on duty.]

Change of Status—Report changes of name, address, or phone to your supervisor.

Lockers—[If you provide them, explain how the employee gets one and how it should be maintained. Discourage employees from bringing valuables to work and leaving them in lockers. Explain that you cannot be responsible for valuables left in lockers.]

Property Removal—We reserve the right to check parcels of employees. Our food and other property may not be removed from the premises, unless you have the written permission of management.

Other Policies—We will be asking you for a work permit if you are a minor. We also require proof that you are at least _____ years old to serve alcoholic beverages in this state. Foreign-born employees may be asked to show us their alien registration card.

Disciplinary Procedures

If you have violated our rules you will receive verbal and/or written warnings, depending on the circumstances. Failure to correct the problem can ultimately lead to discharge.

In the event of a major infraction of our rules, an employee may be subject to immediate discharge without a prior warning. These major infractions include, but are not limited to:

• The use or possession of alcoholic beverages or illegal drugs while on our premises, as well as reporting for work under the influence of alcohol or drugs.

• Unauthorized removal of property.

• Giving away food.

• Fighting or insubordination.

Figure 3-3. *(continued)*

- Possession of a weapon while on the employer's premises.

- Discourtesy or rudeness to guests.

- Punching someone else's time card.

We do hope that none of these situations will occur and that our relationship will be a lasting one.

Separation Procedures

If you decide to terminate your employment with us, we ask your consideration in giving us two weeks' notice so that we may find a suitable replacement. When you leave us, you will have an exit interview to complete any paperwork, collect any monies due, and to discuss your reasons for leaving. Your manager will also tell you how your performance was evaluated. Any information you give on your reasons for leaving will be kept confidential.

In the event of a layoff, usually caused by a slowing of business, you may be eligible for severance pay, depending on your length of employment. [Indicate your specific policy.]

This Is Not a Contract

Nothing said in this handbook implies an employment contract. Employment can be terminated at will by either party.

TOUR AND PERSONAL INTRODUCTIONS

Your manager will give you a tour of the restaurant and introduce you to your co-workers and trainer. If you have any questions at all about any of the policies discussed in this handbook ask your manager. Be sure that you understand all our policies before signing your orientation checklist.

We wish you good luck in your new job and a prosperous career with us!

Figure 3-4. Receipt of personnel handbook.

PLEASE ACKNOWLEDGE RECEIPT OF

_____ **PERSONNEL HANDBOOK**
(restaurant name)

I have received the _____ Personnel Handbook and I know that I am responsible for reading and understanding its contents.

NAME (Print) _____

SIGNATURE _____ DATE _____

It is a good idea to have the employee sign a statement that he or she has read the handbook for the same reasons as signing the checklist. Refer to Figure 3-4 for such a statement.

Follow-up Meetings

Follow-up meetings are periodic discussions you have with the new employee during the first month of employment. Their purpose is to insure that the training is progressing well by communicating how the new employee is doing and by assisting with any problems he or she may be having. These meetings need not be time-consuming—they may often last only ten minutes—but they can serve as an important check on the effectiveness of your training programs and resolve problems before they magnify.

It is recommended that you have a follow-up meeting with the new employee at least once a week until the employee has successfully completed your training program and is "certified" to work a given position in your operation. Call the employee into your office during a quiet time and sit down together. It is not the same simply to shout out, "Hey, Joe, how ya' doin'?" in the work area while the trainee is working. This could hardly be considered a follow-up meeting, because the employee has no chance to say anything.

One of these follow-up meetings should be a formal performance evaluation, done within the first 30 working days. You should also meet with the trainer regularly during the training period to monitor the new employee's progress. Refer to Figure 3-5, sample questions to ask at follow-up meetings with new employees, for suggestions on how to use these meetings for the best results.

The checklist, the personnel handbook, and the follow-up meetings are the basics of an effective orientation program. Here are some additional points on implementing an orientation program in your establishment.

1. Reviewing the orientation checklist may take one or two hours. In more complex operations, orientation can take one-half to one full day, depending on the amount of information to be covered.

2. Pay the trainee for orientation. Do not try to save a few dollars and leave the trainee with the suspicion that you will try to take advantage of employees. Pay the new person for the time you spend reviewing the orientation checklist together.

3. Prepare the trainee for any special circumstances. For example, if you have a temperamental chef, or you become short-tempered at times, or a great many guests arrive all at once, or the employee has to earn seniority before getting the better stations, tell the trainee the circumstances and ask if he or she is willing to accept them. In this way new employees will not be

Figure 3-5. Sample questions to ask at follow-up meetings with new employees.

How do you think your training is progressing?

Are there any areas where you think you can use more practice and would like some assistance?

I'd now like to explain to you how we think you're progressing, pointing out those areas where you're doing very well and those areas which we need to work on. . . .

Do you have any questions or concerns? I'd like to help with anything you don't understand or which causes you problems.

[Also remember to have regular meetings with the trainer so that you are kept informed of the new employee's progress.]

---

surprised with adverse circumstances they had no knowledge of and no intention of accepting. (These issues should be addressed before the employee is hired, but it is a good idea to repeat them and gain the employee's acceptance during orientation.)

4. It is desirable for legal reasons to have signed statements on record that tipped employees understand that they must report 100% of their tips to the IRS and that servers of alcohol know your policies on this issue. Refer to Figure 3-6, alcohol awareness, for one suggested statement on the latter topic. Check with your attorney on the final draft you choose to use. If you do not want employees to become frightened by having to sign so many statements, combine them on one document and ask for the employee's signature only once.

5. Many companies use audiovisual programs to assist in orientating the new employee. When there is a budget to produce them, these programs are recommended. They are most often cost-effective when produced for multiunits of a chain. In such cases the production costs are disseminated among many units.

6. If you are hiring many people during a certain season or prior to opening, you may want to conduct a "welcome meeting" in which you can orientate the entire group at one time. It is nice to serve refreshments at these meetings and to invite top management to attend and meet the employees. Hotels will commonly invite new employees from all departments to a welcome meeting conducted by the personnel department. The individual departments should also give new employees their own orientation, which should be geared to their specific departments and supplement the general information given at the welcome meeting.

Once you have properly orientated the new employees to your operation, you are ready to begin the skills training program. Through orientation, the new employees will have formed a favorable impression of you and your operation, and they will be familiar with your general expectations of them. They are now ready to learn the job for which they were hired.

SUMMARY

Orientation is the act of familiarizing the new employee with the physical layout, with the procedures of the establishment, and with the other workers. Orientation imparts knowledge to the trainee and has a positive effect on motivation. An effective orientation program can be developed consisting of

Figure 3-6. Alcohol awareness.

I understand that as a server of alcoholic beverages I have a legal responsibility to refuse service to anyone under the legal drinking age and to anyone who is already intoxicated.

I will immediately stop serving alcoholic beverages to anyone who exhibits signs of intoxication, such as the following:

slurred speech

difficulty lighting a cigarette

arguing with or annoying other guests

tearfulness

drowsiness

difficulty in focusing eyes

memory loss

spilling drinks

falling or stumbling

difficulty picking up change

I will follow the policies established by management for the responsible service of alcoholic beverages.

NAME (Print) _____

SIGNATURE _____ DATE _____

---

three components: the checklist, the personnel handbook, and the follow-up meetings.

The checklist is an enumeration of all the items you need to explain to the trainee. Its purpose is to aid you in being complete and consistent in your orientation of employees. The checklist can be incorporated into a more detailed document, the staff file folder. This folder is a compact way of recording a great deal of information about the employee.

The handbook is a written explanation of the points on the orientation checklist that you verbally explain to the new employee. It is written for the trainee to read and greatly increases the amount of details the trainee will remember.

Follow-up meetings are periodic discussions that you have with the new employee during the first weeks of employment. Their purpose is to insure that the employee's training is progressing well by communicating how he or she is doing and by assisting with any problems the newcomer may be having. You should have regular meetings with the trainer, as well, to monitor the new employee's progress. It is also advisable to have a formal performance evaluation during the first 30 working days.

Give the new employee a copy of the personnel handbook at the time of hire and ask that it be read prior to orientation. Set aside one or two hours to explain every item on the orientation checklist with the new employee. Then monitor the newcomer's progress through periodic follow-up meetings during the first month of employment.

The orientation checklist, staff file folder, personnel handbook, follow-up meeting questions, and statements for the employee to sign, included in this chapter, should be used as guidelines in developing your own orientation program.

PART THREE

JOB ANALYSIS

4

Breaking a Job into Tasks

In the next two chapters, we will be concerned with analyzing a job in order to define the tasks that have to be performed and to describe how they should be performed. Job analysis is the first step in preparing a skills training program: It is the identification of the tasks an employee must perform in the job and the steps the employee must take to complete each task. A task, in this context, refers to a portion of work assigned to a person as part of his or her job responsibilities. When the job analysis is completed, you will be ready to train your employees. So, the first step is the identification and specification of the job in all its details, and the next step is the communication of the job to the trainee.

Every job consists of a series of tasks. For example, consider the "job" of playing tennis. What are some of the tasks one would have to grasp in order to play tennis? One would have to learn how to hold the racket, serve the ball, return serve, make forehand shots, make backhand shots, lob, volley, and so forth. Or take the job of driving a car. Some of the tasks included in this job are starting the car, operating the gears, driving forward, going in reverse, turning, and parking.

Breaking the job down into tasks is essential for both trainer and trainee. An entire job is too complex to be taught or grasped directly, so it needs to be presented as a series of tasks. Breaking the job down into smaller segments makes it possible for the trainer to teach and for the trainee to learn the job.

Job Checklists

A job checklist is a listing of the tasks to be performed, as well as the knowledge needed to perform the tasks of a particular job. In order to give a complete picture of the employee's training and job performance, the checklist should also record the scores on any tests and performance evaluations given as part of the training program. A checklist should be prepared for each job in your restaurant, similar to the job checklists for a server and a cashier given in Figures 4-1 and 4-2, respectively.

(Text continued on p. 51)

Figure 4-1. Job checklist—server. (Courtesy of Hospitality Industry Training, Inc.)

The server's job is to serve the guests in a prompt and courteous manner in accordance with the rules of good service, and to practice suggestive selling techniques to build sales and enhance the guests' enjoyment. The server is also responsible for handling cash properly and for performing opening and closing tasks as assigned. The servers supervise the bus staff.

Name of Employee _____

Reports to _____ Date Started this Job _____

Trainer: Place a check next to each task when the trainee has mastered it.

General Considerations	**Performance Evaluation**
_____ Appearance	A-B-C-F
_____ Conduct at work	A-B-C-F
_____ Hospitality and courtesy toward guests	A-B-C-F
_____ Attendance/punctuality	A-B-C-F
_____ Other _____	A-B-C-F
Opening Duties and Side Work	A-B-C-F

_____ Station and table numbers
_____ Folding napkins
_____ Placing tablecloths on tables
_____ Setting tables
_____ Stocking stations
_____ Cleaning and marrying condiments
_____ Refilling salt and pepper shakers
_____ Refilling sugar bowls
_____ Other _____

Service A-B-C-F

_____ The overall sequence of service
_____ Pouring water at the table
_____ Numbering guests at the table
_____ Greeting guests and taking the cocktail order
_____ Filling the cocktail order at the service bar
_____ Serving cocktails
_____ Taking the order for appetizers and the main course
_____ Suggesting wine
_____ Ordering and picking up appetizers
_____ Serving appetizers
_____ Clearing and resetting the table after appetizers
_____ Serving bread and butter
_____ Ordering and picking up wine
_____ Serving wine
_____ Ordering and picking up the main course
_____ Serving the main course
_____ Clearing and crumbing the table after the main course
_____ Suggesting dessert, coffee, and after-dinner drinks
_____ Serving desserts
_____ Serving coffee, tea, and after-dinner-drinks
_____ Presenting the check and closing service

Clearing and Resetting the Table A-B-C-F

_____ Stacking items on a bus tray
_____ Carrying a bus tray
_____ Emptying a bus tray by the dish machine
_____ Clearing the table and changing the tablecloth after guests have left
_____ Resetting tables for the next seating

Handling Guest Checks A-B-C-F

_____ Obtaining guest checks at the start of service
_____ Explanation of register keyboard and commands
_____ Opening a check
_____ Entering items on the guest check
_____ Tallying the check at the end of service
_____ Paying the guest check

Product Knowledge A-B-C-F

_____ Menu—description and taste of every item on the menu
_____ Wine—background info, description and taste of wines on the wine list, recommending wines with food
_____ Cocktails/liquor—brands stocked, preparation, service, and taste of popular cocktails and specialty drinks
_____ Policies on responsible service of alcohol

Figure 4-1. *(continued)*

Suggestive Selling   A-B-C-F

_____ Suggestive selling techniques
_____ Sales per guest of $_____ meet or exceed restaurant ave-
          rage of $_____

Closing Duties and Side Work   A-B-C-F

_____ Washing service trays
_____ Cleaning wine buckets
_____ Cleaning side stations
_____ Other _____
_____
_____

Other Responsibilities   A-B-C-F

_____

_____

_____

Quiz/Test Scores (90% is minimum passing score)

Menu quiz _____%   Wine/liquor quiz _____%
Service quiz _____%

Training

I have placed a check mark before each task that I have taught the trainee. I am satisfied that he or she can perform each task correctly.

_____   _____   _____
Signature of Trainer   Signature of Manager   Date

Performance Evaluations

Use this form for periodic performance evaluations. Use as many lines as necessary to indicate your comments.

Code: A = Excellent
        B = Good, but can still improve
        C = Borderline performance, improvement is required
        F = Unsatisfactory

Date	Overall Rating	Comments of Manager and Employee	Initials Employee	Manager

Figure 4-2. Job checklist—cashier. (Courtesy of Hospitality Industry Training, Inc.)

The cashier's job is to ring up the guests' purchases and to accept payment at the end of the cafeteria line. The cashier is expected to serve the guests in a prompt and courteous manner and to handle cash in accordance with established procedures.

Name of Employee _____

Reports to _____ Date Started this Job _____

Trainer: Place a check next to each task when the trainee has mastered it.

General Considerations	**Performance Evaluation**
_____ Appearance	A–B–C–F
_____ Conduct at work	A–B–C–F
_____ Courtesy toward guests	A–B–C–F
_____ Attendance/punctuality	A–B–C–F

Figure 4-2. *(continued)*

Guest Relations   A-B-C-F

_____ Serving guests in a friendly manner
_____ Answering commonly asked questions
_____ Handling complaints

Menu Knowledge   A-B-C-F

_____ Recognizing menu items on guest's tray
_____ Prices
_____ Policy on substitutions

Preparing for Service   A-B-C-F

_____ Obtaining and counting your bank
_____ Setting up the cash drawer

Operating the Register   A-B-C-F

_____ Understanding the keyboard
_____ Ringing up a sale
_____ Using the TOTAL button
_____ Using AMOUNT TENDERED
_____ Voiding a transaction
_____ Canceling a transaction
_____ Accuracy at working the register
_____ Speed at working the register

Handling Cash   A-B-C-F

_____ Counting change for the guest
_____ Handling employee meal discounts
_____ Handling promotional coupons
_____ Spotting and handling counterfeit bills
_____ Spotting and handling quick-change artists
_____ Policy on travelers checks, personal checks, and credit cards

Closing Service   A-B-C-F

_____ Closing the register and counting your money
_____ Filling out a bank report
_____ Returning your bank to the manager
_____ Safeguarding against theft

Quiz Scores (90% is minimum passing score)

Menu quiz _____% 　　Cashier quiz _____%

Training

I have placed a check mark before each task that I have taught the trainee. I am satisfied that he or she can perform each task correctly.

_____   _____
Signature of Trainer   Signature of Manager

Date _____

Performance Evaluations

Use this form for periodic performance evaluations. Use as many lines as necessary to indicate your comments.

Code: A = Excellent
            B = Good, but can still improve
            C = Borderline performance, improvement is required
            F = Unsatisfactory

Date	Overall Rating	Comments of Manager and Employee	Initials

The checklist indicates the specific tasks of the job under broader categories of responsibility. For example, folding napkins and setting tables are two tasks of servers listed under the broader category of "opening duties and side work." Ringing up a sale and using the total button are two tasks of cashiers listed under "operating the register."

The checklist may also specify information needed to perform each task, such as knowledge of the menu and the wine list for servers. This one form, the job checklist, can serve three useful purposes to you. It can be used as an aid in: (1) hiring, (2) training, and (3) maintaining performance standards.

Hiring

The job checklist can be used as a job description. You can show and explain it to applicants, so they will understand the responsibilities of the job. In addition, the listing of tasks can be useful to you in identifying the qualifications you are seeking in applicants for the job.

More common types of job descriptions only indicate broad categories of responsibility without listing every task. Because these job descriptions lack sufficient detail, they are not useful in training, but they do give a broad overview of the job to applicants or newly hired employees.

The checklists given in this chapter indicate broad categories of responsibility, as well as specific tasks, so these same forms can be useful in giving a general overview of the job and in teaching specific tasks.

Training

The checklist is indispensable to the trainer in assuring that the training is organized and complete. The checklist provides a list of all the items the trainer must teach the trainee and a method of checking off items as the trainee masters them. The checklist gives a concise visual record of the entire training program and the trainee's progress through it. The checklist is also helpful to the trainee, because it describes what he or she will be learning.

In order to use the checklists given in this chapter, the trainer should place a check mark to the left of each item when the trainee masters it. The trainer should also record the trainee's score on any quizzes or tests given. The A-B-C-F rating system on the right side of the form should be used for evaluating performance after the trainee has been shown all the tasks of the job and has started working independently. When all items are covered and the training is completed, the trainer should sign the form and give it to the manager for signing, indicating that the trainee is "certified" to perform the job.

Maintaining Performance Standards

It is important to periodically evaluate the performance of employees if the training is to have a lasting effect. The checklist also serves as a performance evaluation form and has advantages over the more common types of performance evaluations. Using the checklist for performance evaluations allows you to focus on the employee's specific actions or behavior, rather than solely on the qualities commonly evaluated on "trait scales," such as quality and quantity of work, initiative, and cooperation. Using the job checklist for performance evaluation allows you to have a custom-designed form for each job category, based on the performance of tasks, and thereby to better focus on the employee's actions.

Evaluate each employee's performance within the first 30 working days and quarterly thereafter. For each category, circle A, B, C, or F. The ratings are similar to school grades: A = excellent; B = good, but can still improve; C = borderline performance, improvement is required; and F = unsatisfactory. Make specific comments about the employee's performance on the form. Arrive at an overall rating of A, B, C, or F for the employee. The overall rating may not be a simple average of the ratings in each category, as the categories may be unequal in importance to you. Discuss the evaluation with the employee and follow-up on any corrective action needed to make the employee's performance good to excellent in all categories. (More will be said about evaluating performance in Chapter 10, Monitoring Performance.)

In summary, the development of the job checklist is the first step in a successful skills training program. It breaks a job down into tasks. Moreover, a well-designed checklist is also useful as a job description, overall training record, and performance evaluation form.

Use the two job checklists given in this chapter as guidelines in developing checklists for each position in your operation.

Considerations for Preparing Job Checklists

Identify Tasks

The first thing to do in developing a job checklist is to list every task or activity that is part of a particular job. Let your mind pour out every item it can think of that is an aspect of the job in question. Another way to arrive at a listing of tasks is to ask each person doing the job to write a list of all of the tasks, then compare and combine the lists to form the job checklist. A third alternative, and often the best method of composing your job checklist, is to trail someone who is performing the job and write down every task he or she performs during a shift.

Categorize Tasks

Once you have a list of all of the activities, aspects, or tasks of a job, categorize the entries. Do some of the items fall under one general heading? If so, group them. For example, on the server checklist, items such as setting tables, folding napkins, placing tablecloths on the tables, and stocking stations are all categorized as being part of "opening duties and side work." Items such as counting change, handling coupons, and spotting counterfeit bills appear on the cashier checklist under the category of "handling cash." The categories or groups identify major job responsibilities and are helpful in organizing the job for teaching.

Broaden and Narrow Tasks as Necessary

Take another look at the tasks or items listed. Are some of them too broad or too narrow? The tasks should represent small sections of the job that could be taught in 15- to 30-minute training sessions. For example, if you have a very sophisticated restaurant, "taking the order" would be too broad to be considered a task in your restaurant. This item should be further broken down into taking cocktail, wine, main course, and dessert orders. However, if you operate a fast-food restaurant with a simplified menu and service, "taking the order" may describe one simple task.

An example of an item that is too narrow is "presenting the check to the host." There is not much to be said about this, except to indicate when and how the check should be presented, such as, "When the host requests the bill, place the guest check face-down on a tip tray to the right of the host." This is merely a step in the closing of service and should be broadened to "presenting the check and closing service." The broader task would include when and how to present the check, as well as accepting payment from the guest, bringing change or credit card voucher for signing, and thanking guests for their visit. On the cashier checklist, "closing the register" is grouped with "counting your money" as one task, because in this operation closing the register only requires calling the manager to lock the register, so it is too narrow to be defined as a task by itself.

As a general rule of thumb, tasks on your checklist should contain between 6 and 20 steps. If they contain fewer than 6 steps, chances are they are being defined too narrowly and should be combined with related activities to make a broader entry. If a task is too narrowly defined, the job is fragmentized into unnecessarily small segments, which can confuse the trainee and prolong the training. If your entries contain more than 20 steps, they probably should be broken down further, as too many steps presented at one time can also confuse the trainee.

Determine How Detailed to Make Checklist

The degree to which you need to break down the job depends on two factors: the complexity of your operation and the knowledge or experience of a typical new employee. For example, if you have a simple wine list of six to eight wines, then you can have one entry on your checklist called "knowledge of wines—pronunciation, taste, and description of each wine on the wine list." However, if you sell 100 different wines, then the wine training of the staff becomes much more complex. Wine then becomes a major category on the checklist, with a number of headings under it.

Another factor in determining how much you need to break down the job is the context of knowledge of a typical employee who is hired for the job. A hotel chain that opened properties in underdeveloped countries and hired local people found that it once had a waiter on the floor for three days before anyone realized he was not wearing shoes! Even in the United States, if you are hiring the young and inexperienced, it is best to go into great detail.

Recognize Options in Listing Tasks

There are many options in listing and grouping tasks on your checklists, so do not search for the one perfect way—often there may be more than one right way. On the server checklist, serving wine is listed under the category "service." It could also have been listed under wine in the category "product knowledge." The training could be effective using either type of classification. The details of the job should be covered in some logical order, although there may be some options in the way the tasks are defined and grouped.

Include Information

Include information needed to perform each task, as well as the tasks themselves. Not every entry on the checklist represents a physical activity the trainee must perform. Some entries represent knowledge necessary to perform the tasks properly. Although we refer to the checklist as a listing of tasks, do not be reluctant to include indispensable information that will improve the performance of the tasks.

Include "General Considerations"

Include "general considerations" on the checklist, such as appearance and attendance, so the form can be used as an overall performance evaluation. Also include a rating scale, such as A-B-C-F, for evaluating performance.

Include Test Scores

Include test scores, if these are part of your training program, so all aspects of the training will be recorded on the checklist.

Include Tests for Speed When Necessary

If tasks have to be completed within a specified time, tests for speed should also be included in the employee's training and indicated on the checklist.

Consider Indicating a Training Schedule

Some companies arrange the checklist in the order in which the tasks are taught. These checklists indicate days and hours of the day in which the tasks are to be taught; hence they also serve as the training schedule. This is another option you may want to consider.

Revise Checklists

Revise your checklists periodically. Start with something workable, then as you use it, refine it. Add tasks you had forgotten. Further break down tasks that are too broad. Review your checklists periodically and update them as job responsibilities change.

Use a Word Processor

If possible, use a word processor to prepare the checklists as well as all other training materials. The ease with which material can be prepared and revised with a word processor is incomparable. Many, many hours of your time will be saved by having one.

SUMMARY

Before you can teach someone a job, it is necessary to break the job down into tasks and to break each task into steps. A task is a portion of work assigned to a person as part of his or her job responsibilities. A job checklist is the breakdown of a job into its tasks.

A well-designed checklist can aid the manager in hiring, training, and maintaining performance standards of employees. The checklist should group tasks under broader categories of job responsibility, so it can be used to describe the job in broader terms to applicants and new employees without going into each task. For training, a check should be placed in front of each task when the trainee masters it. If the trainee is given any written tests, the scores should be recorded on the checklist. When a rating scale is included for each job category, the checklist can also be used for evaluating the employee's performance on a regular basis after the training is completed.

Using the sample checklists given in this chapter, prepare job checklists for each position in your operation.

5

Breaking Tasks into Steps and Writing a Training Manual

In Chapter 4, we said that every job consists of a series of tasks. This list of tasks answers the question, "What do you want the trainee to do?" For example, assume you hire a busperson. What do you want the busperson to do? The answer is the list of tasks that comprise the job, such as setting up the side stations, pouring water for the guests, bringing bread and butter to the table, and clearing the table.

Each task, in turn, consists of a series of steps. For example, some of the steps involved in bringing bread and butter to the table may include lining a bread basket with a napkin, placing a variety of rolls in the basket, placing butter curls in the butter dish, and serving the bread and butter to the table. When you have identified the steps comprising each task, you have answered the question, "How do you want the trainee to perform?" The tasks identify what you want done, and the steps identify how you want the tasks done. It is necessary to identify both the tasks and the steps to performing each task before you can properly train someone to do the job.

The Importance of Specifying the Steps

If you do not specify how you want each task performed, new employees will be forced to decide the steps for themselves. They have to function, so they must perform the tasks using *some* method. The only question is, will they perform using the steps you have clearly defined and shown them, or will they have to decide the steps for themselves because these steps were not indicated in the training program? For example, if you do not specify how the waiter should prepare the dinner salad, he will have to fill in the details for himself, perhaps overportioning the ingredients, drowning the salad in dressing, or neglecting to serve the salad on a chilled plate. There are many things that can go wrong in the execution of any task. After a certain number of repetitions of the right way or the wrong way, work habits are formed. By showing new employees how to perform each task in detail, step by step, you will be instituting good work habits that will improve your bottom line in countless ways.

The Difficulty in Identifying the Steps

It can often be difficult to break a task down into its steps, especially for someone who knows the task very well. The problem is that once we master a task, the steps become automatized and we perform the task without being consciously aware of the steps we use. For example, small children struggle over the most basic tasks, such as buttoning a shirt. It would be extremely difficult for an adult to identify the steps necessary to button a shirt, because this task, once mastered, is performed automatically. It usually takes a conscious effort to reconstruct the steps so that one can do a good job of teaching someone a task. It is very helpful to identify the steps comprising a task while you are actually doing the task or while you are watching someone else do the task.

The Benefits of Putting the Steps in Writing

There are great benefits to having the steps in writing rather than only in your mind.

It Benefits the Operator

One has to be far more precise in writing something down than in just explaining it verbally. The act of writing down the procedures for performing a job also clarifies and standardizes those procedures in your own mind. Many times you will be establishing your procedures and policies when you write your training manuals.

Writing down procedures also makes them "official." There can be no mistake about your standards when they are in writing. The reason all laws are written is that writing makes them objective, rather than merely thoughts in someone's mind.

It Benefits the Trainer

There is a need to delegate training to supervisors and hourly employees, because the operator usually does not have time to personally train new employees. How do you delegate training while still maintaining control? One essential way is to put your policies in writing. Written policies aid you in controlling the training in two ways: (1) They guide your trainer in providing step-by-step instruction. As we said earlier, it is difficult to break a task into steps. The written procedures give the trainer the steps needed to properly teach the trainee. (2) Written policies encourage the trainer to use your methods rather than his or her own. In order to be speaking for you, your trainer needs your written guidelines. With your written instructions to follow, the trainer has less temptation and justification for teaching his or her own methods.

It Benefits the Trainee

All employees except those with poor reading skills can benefit from written instruction. Written aids allow you to place more of the burden of training on the trainees. They do not have to depend solely on someone's verbally feeding information to them. The training becomes partly self-instructional with written procedures. (Placing more of the burden of training on trainees also makes the trainer's job easier, which is especially important when there are a great number of persons to train, such as in seasonal operations or during openings.)

Written aids also have the advantage of greatly enhancing the trainee's understanding and retention. There is too much information for the trainee to remember. If everything is taught verbally without any written aids, the trainee will forget many of the details. Having written procedures will enable the trainee to preview information before it is taught by the trainer and also to review the same information after it is taught.

Writing a Training Manual

When the procedures for performing the job are put in writing, the result is a training manual. The most important concern in writing a training manual is clarity. More important than glossy pages, fancy covers, typeset text, or color photos is clarity. Above all else, the reader should find the information clear, which means that it should be well organized, logical, and understandable. If, in addition to being clear, the material is also attractively assembled, it is certainly an advantage. However, clarity is the most important consideration, and in this respect, small independent operations can have training manuals that are every bit as effective as those of the major chains.

There are two prime considerations in making your training manuals clear: organization and content of material.

The Organization of the Manual
Decide on the Basic Organization

The basic organization is usually by position, such as a server manual, host manual, or prep cook manual. It usually makes the most sense to organize the manual by position, because employees are most often hired and trained for specific positions. A variation on this kind of organization is to group related positions for which you frequently cross-train, such as grouping the dishwasher's and busperson's jobs together in one manual. Or you may want to have one manual for back-of-the-house and another for front-of-the-house positions. In this case, the separate job positions become the main sections in the manual, rather than manuals in their own right. For example, one company has a manual for the front of the house with three sections for busser, server, and host. Its back-of-the-house manual has four sections for the four positions of broiler cook, fry cook, prep cook, and dishwasher.

Sometimes, the manual may be organized in terms of phases of training. For example, one operation that has different rooms and serves buffet style as well as from a menu has its server manual arranged in the following sections: busperson, buffet server, Terrace server, and Gold Room server, corresponding to the phases of training a new server completes. The server starts as either a busser or a buffet server. In either case, the manager considers it essential that the servers know the busser's job, so he includes the busser section in the server training manual. When servers demonstrate skill, they are promoted to Terrace servers, where they serve from a menu in another room of the operation. Some servers are further promoted to the Gold Room, which is the formal dining room.

If the basic organization is chosen carefully, it will greatly add to the clarity of the manual.

Have a Table of Contents

The table of contents should essentially be the listing of tasks from the job checklist. It is these tasks that you are going to explain in the manual. If the job checklist is done well, it will give the manual a well-organized structure. The table of contents explains the manual's organization to the trainee.

Figures 5-1 and 5-2 show the tables of contents for manuals from two fast-food operations, Nature's Pantry, a healthy food restaurant, and the

Figure 5-1. Nature's Pantry's fast-food server training manual: table of contents. (Courtesy of Inhilco, Inc.)

FAST-FOOD SERVER TRAINING MANUAL

TABLE OF CONTENTS

Figure 5-2. The Grill's cook training manual: table of contents. (Courtesy of Inhilco, Inc.)

COOK TRAINING MANUAL

TABLE OF CONTENTS

Grill, a hamburgerie. The tables of contents are for the server manual at Nature's Pantry and the cook manual at the Grill. (The training materials given in this chapter are from Inhilco, Inc., of New York. Some of them have been slightly modified to demonstrate the points made in this chapter.)

Include a Welcome Message

Consider including a welcome message at the beginning of the manual, which acquaints the new employee with the job. Figure 5-3 shows the message that begins the server manual for Nature's Pantry.

Number the Pages

Numbering the pages makes it easier to locate material in the manual.

Design a Special Heading for the Pages

Design a heading for pages in the manual that distinguishes them from any other pages from any other document. Use your company logo in the design, if possible. Refer to the procedures given in this chapter for a simply designed heading that indicates the title of the procedure, the position, the department, the page number, and the date. When procedures are updated, replace them with the updated versions and revise the date.

Begin Each Task on a New Page

When a procedure is finished, begin the next one on a new page. In this way, the tasks the trainees are studying are made very clear to them.

Subdivide the Material

You may want to use index tabs to separate main sections of the manual. Break up the more complex procedures with subheadings to aid the trainee in finding information and in following the procedures. Refer to the procedures for how to prepare sandwiches and how to cook french fries, from the Nature's Pantry and Grill manuals in Figures 5-4 and 5-5, respectively, for examples of using subheadings within procedures.

(Text continued on p. 71)

Figure 5-3. The welcome message that begins the server manual for Nature's Pantry. (Courtesy of Inhilco, Inc.)

WELCOME TO NATURE'S PANTRY

Nature's Pantry is part of the Big Kitchen, and like the other restaurants in the World Trade Center, it is operated by Inhilco, Inc. Our company is a subsidiary of Hilton International.

The orientation booklet you received tells you something about Nature's Pantry, the Big Kitchen, and our other food facilities. The Big Kitchen consists of eight restaurants and four retail stores, each with a unique menu and style. It is designed like a marketplace, similar to the markets that once flourished on this very site in lower Manhattan many years ago.

Nature's Pantry is a healthy food restaurant with an adjacent retail store. The restaurant consists of a sandwich-and-salad bar, a juice bar, and a frozen yogurt station. Nature's Pantry opens at 11:30 A.M. The sandwich-and-salad bar closes at 2:30 P.M. while the other stations remain open until 8 P.M.

At the sandwich-and-salad bar guests can get salads of fresh fruit and vegetables combined with cheese, poultry, or fish, and stone-ground whole wheat sandwiches with garnitures of alfalfa sprouts, currants, shredded celery, and shredded carrots. Soup of the day, a steamed vegetable, and homemade peanut butter are also available.

For beverages, the fruit bar serves fruits and vegetables juiced to order, thick fruit and yogurt shakes, and herbal teas. For dessert or snacks, the popular yogurt station has frozen yogurt garnished with fruit, wheat germ, granola, nuts, and raisins.

As a server in Nature's Pantry, you will be required to serve the guest, as well as set up, maintain, and clean your station and handle cash. (The handling of cash is covered in a separate manual.)

Most of our guests are people who work at or near the World Trade Center. Because these people have limited time for meals, the service in Nature's Pantry is fast, yet efficient and excellent in quality. We expect you to meet our high standards of job performance and, above all, to always be courteous and gracious to our valued guests.

This manual explains the tasks you will be required to do. By studying it and practicing the procedures, you will acquire the skill necessary to perform your job excellently.

Figure 5-4. How to prepare sandwiches. (Courtesy of Inhilco, Inc.)

INHILCO TRAINING

HOW TO PREPARE SANDWICHES	POSITION Server	DATE 12/20/77
	DEPARTMENT Nature's Pantry	PAGE 14

Be sure the Nature's Pantry bain marie has been properly set up before service so that you have all the ingredients necessary to make sandwiches.

Ingredients

The ingredients for sandwiches are listed in the order in which they are placed on the plate:

Tuna Salad

2 slices bread
1 oz. shredded carrots
4 oz. tuna salad
1 slice tomato
1 oz. dressing
½ oz. alfalfa sprouts
1 lemon wedge (⅙ of lemon)

Turkey Salad

2 slices bread
1 oz. shredded carrots
4 oz. turkey-apple salad
1 slice tomato
1 oz. dressing
½ oz. currants
½ oz. walnuts

Peanut Butter

2 slices bread
2 oz. peanut butter
1 oz. apricot butter
4 oz. cut fruit
1 oz. shredded carrots
½ oz. currants

The following procedure will be explained for the tuna sandwich. Follow the same procedure for the other sandwiches as well.

Place the Bread on the Plate

1. Lay the 2 slices of stone-ground whole wheat bread on top of each other in an entree plate.

2. With a sharp knife, cut the top slice (only) in half vertically.

Figure 5-4. *(continued)*

INHILCO TRAINING

	POSITION Server	DATE 12/20/77
HOW TO PREPARE SANDWICHES	DEPARTMENT Nature's Pantry	PAGE 15

3. Put the 2 halves alongside the uncut slice on the plate, one half on each side, with the cut side facing out. (See the diagram below.)

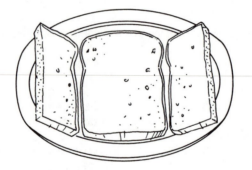

Place the Food on the Bread

4. Using the small tongs, put a pinch of shredded carrots on top of the uncut slice of bread.

5. With the 3-oz. scoop, place one heaping scoop of tuna salad over the carrots and spread the tuna out over the uncut slice.

6. Put 1 slice of tomato over the tuna.

7. Pour one 1-oz. ladle of parsley-yogurt dressing over the tomato.

8. With small tongs, place 1 pinch of alfalfa sprouts on top.

9. Using tongs, pick up 1 lemon wedge and put it on the side of the sandwich.

Note: This is an open-faced sandwich, so leave the 2 halves of bread where they are on the plate.

Serve

10. Serve the sandwich to the guest with knife, fork, and napkin.

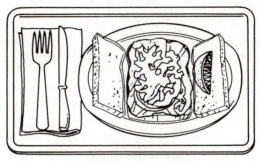

Finished Sandwich

Figure 5-5. How to cook french fries. (Courtesy of Inhilco, Inc.)

INHILCO TRAINING

	POSITION Cook	DATE 1/16/78
HOW TO COOK FRENCH FRIES		
	DEPARTMENT Grill	PAGE 27

Set the Fryer

1. Turn the fryolator on about 30 minutes before lunch begins to allow the grease to warm.

2. Be sure the dial is set at 350 degrees F. Using a probe thermometer, be sure the temperature is at 350 degrees F., adjusting the dial as necessary.

3. Be sure the shortening in the kettle is up to ½ inch of the fill mark.

Put the Fries In

4. Fill the basket ¼ to ⅓ full with frozen fries. Fill the basket over the counter and not over the grease to prevent the fries from falling into the kettle. Do not fill the basket more than ¼ to ⅓ full because the fries will fall out into the grease. Too many fried will also lower the temperature of the grease and cook improperly.

Figure 5-5. *(continued)*

If fries do fall into the grease, promptly remove them with a skimmer to preserve the life of the shortening.

5. Place the basket of fries into the grease. This should be done immediately because the fries should not be given time to thaw. The fries must be frozen in order to produce a good-quality product.

6. Gently shake the basket to level out the fries. Be sure they are completely immersed in the shortening.

Cook

7. Cook for approximately 3–3½ minutes. The fries should be lightly browned, crisp on the outside, and moist on the inside.

Drain

8. When the fries are done, lift the basket, shake it vigorously two to three times and hang it over the shortening to drain for about 15–20 seconds. This is done to remove the excess shortening from the fries. Do not leave the fries over the shortening too long because they will become limp and greasy.

INHILCO TRAINING

HOW TO COOK FRENCH FRIES	POSITION Cook	DATE 1/16/78
	DEPARTMENT Grill	PAGE 28

Remove the Fries from the Basket

9. Empty the basket of fries into a perforated hotel pan. The pan must be peforated so the grease can drip out.

10. Place the fries under the fry warmer. Do not hold the fries longer than 10 minutes before serving. You should not make more fries than you can sell in 10 minutes. During slow periods, fry to order.

Note: Never refry french fries. Be sure you are serving the best-quality product to our valued guests.

Give Credit to the Trainers

Consider including a credit line for trainers who help you prepare the procedures. This gives them recognition for their work.

Have the Manual Professionally Typed

The manual should be professionally typed with no typos, spelling errors, cross-outs, and so on. The trainee gets the impression that the manager is organized and competent if the manual looks professional. It is also easier to read. Consider using a word processor for assembling the manual, because the time saved in preparing and updating the manual can be quite significant. Because of the ease of making changes in the text, a word processor will also improve your writing.

If there is a budget for it and if you do not expect too many revisions in the near future, consider having the manual typeset for an attractive, professional finish.

Consider using a loose-leaf binder for the cover. Although expensive, a loose-leaf allows you to revise individual pages without having to redo the whole manual. In order to prevent the loss of expensive training materials, you may want to set up a quiet place in your restaurant for training where employees can read and/or view your training materials on the premises.

The Content of the Manual
Explain Each Task in a Step-by-Step Manner

Do not be too concise. It is usually best to write in full English sentences, so your exact meaning will be clear. The reason is that sentences express complete thoughts; there is a subject that acts and a verb that describes the action. It will clarify the trainee's thinking if instructions are written in whole sentences. The procedures at the end of the chapter demonstrate this approach.

Various types of tables, checklists, or recipes may be written in an abbreviated style without using full English sentences. Certain kinds of material are best presented this way, such as listings of glassware and the drinks served in each type of glass, shown in Figure 5-6. Tables and lists are fine, provided the material is clearly presented: Columns must be properly labeled and explained: Checklists must indicate what should be done, when, by whom, and so forth. These kinds of materials may form part of the manual; however, shorthand, tabular material should not constitute the entire manual.

A three-column format for writing training procedures is not recommended.

Figure 5-6. Chart of glassware. (Courtesy of Inhilco, Inc.)

INHILCO TRAINING

CHART OF GLASSWARE	POSITION Server	DATE 2/22/80
	DEPARTMENT Windows on the World —The Restaurant	PAGE 19

The chart of glassware indicates the proper glass to use for cocktails.

GLASS		ABBREVIATION FOR GLASS	COCKTAILS (examples)
White wine		WW	White wine Perrier water Spritzer Campari and soda Sherry on the rocks
Red wine		RW	Lillet Red wine Kir
Shot glass			Garnishes (lemon, lime wedges, lemon twist, olives, pearl onions) Shots of whiskey
Rock glass		RCK	Sour/martini on the rocks Gimlet on the rocks Old-fashioned on the rocks All whiskeys on the rocks
Highball glass		HB	Beer Gin and tonic Scotch & soda Screwdriver Other highballs
Collins		COL	Soda Tom Collins Iced tea & coffee Milk

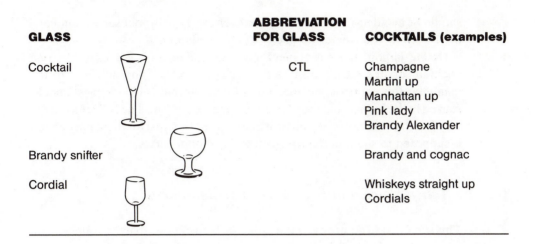

GLASS	ABBREVIATION FOR GLASS	COCKTAILS (examples)
Cocktail	CTL	Champagne Martini up Manhattan up Pink lady Brandy Alexander
Brandy snifter		Brandy and cognac
Cordial		Whiskeys straight up Cordials

These columns are usually headed (1) what to do, (2) how to do it, and (3) why (or remarks). It can be a contrived and cumbersome way to write and to read material. Reasons why and explanatory remarks can easily be indicated in procedures written in a prose form. They should be indicated as they are needed. It is unnecessary and laborious to indicate the reason why or explanatory remarks after every single step is performed, as many of these three-column formats require. In writing procedures, you should let common sense prevail rather than trying to conform the writing to preconceived molds that do not fit the purpose.

The degree to which you have to break down tasks depends on two factors: how demanding you are about how the task should be performed and the state of knowledge of a typical employee. For example, preparing the dinner salad may be a simple procedure if it is done in the back of the house and brought out to the guest, while the procedure may change markedly if the salad is to be prepared tableside. Or if you hire cooks who are graduates of a culinary college, you will not have to go into as much detail about basic cooking procedures as you would if you hired untrained high school students as cooks. Your manuals should reflect the detail necessary to train in your operation, based on your standards and on the kind of people you typically hire. (Once when training young, inexperienced employees to operate a fast-food counter, I told them to put ice in all cold drinks. Later, I found one of them putting ice in the beer! When you are dealing with the young and inexperienced, do not assume anything. Indicate what you want clearly and in detail.)

Use Simple Language

If you were, for example, giving instructions for entering data in the register, it would be unclear to say, "Index your server number." (Computer jargon should be avoided.) Simpler language, such as "Type in your server number," or "Punch in your server number," would be clearer.

Define jargon that newcomers may not understand. For example, one cocktail server's manual repeatedly refers to "NT's," and nowhere in the manual is this expression explained, it turns out that NT's are guest checks started in the lounge and transferred to the dining room. The NT refers to the fact that the cocktail server has not been tipped (no tips) for these parties and is supposed to share in the tip given to the dinner server.

Use the Active Voice and Use Imperative Sentences

This sentence structure casts the procedures in actions that the trainee must take. Its form is one that directs the trainee to take action. For example, the imperative sentence in the active voice, "Pour the wine for the guests" is preferable to the passive voice, "The wine is then poured for the guests," because the former is a command directing the trainee's actions.

Use Pictures to Clarify Your Message

Diagrams or line drawings are excellent for showing many things, such as the setup of areas, the parts of equipment, and the table setting. See how much easier it is to understand the procedure in Figure 5-7, showing "how to make coffee in the Cory coffee maker," with the aid of a small drawing of the machine? Also, refer to the diagram of the lunch setup of Nature's Pantry in Figure 5-8. The setup of this area would be very difficult to understand without a diagram.

For menu items, create a separate book showing a photograph of each menu item as it should appear on the plate, accompanied by a listing of the ingredients, portioning, and preparation of the item. Put the photographs in plastic sheets to protect them from spills.

Getting the Training Manual Written

Once you have decided to write a training manual, the big job is translating your wish into reality. Here are two suggestions.

Select a Writer

If you are not a good writer or if you simply do not have the time, delegate the job of writing the manual to someone else, either a manager, an hourly

Figure 5-7. How to make coffee in the Cory coffee maker. (Courtesy of Inhilco, Inc.)

INHILCO TRAINING

HOW TO MAKE COFFEE IN THE CORY COFFEE MAKER	POSITION Server	DATE 2/9/78
	DEPARTMENT Rotisserie	PAGE 16

Materials Needed

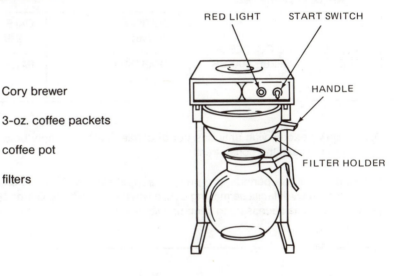

Cory brewer

3-oz. coffee packets

coffee pot

filters

1. Remove the filter holder from the machine by holding the handle and sliding it off.

2. Examine the filter holder. If a used filter is in it, discard the filter and grinds. Be sure the filter holder is clean and free of grinds.

3. Place *one* filter in the filter holder. (Be sure you have only *one* filter, otherwise the water will not get through and will back up and spill over.)

4. Open one 3-oz. bag of coffee and pour it into the filter.

5. Slide the filter holder back onto the machine.

6. Place a clean, empty coffee pot on the warmer directly under the filter holder.

7. Turn the switch to START. Be sure the coffee pot is in place when the switch is turned on, because coffee will immediately begin dripping out of the filter holder.

8. Keep the coffee pot in place until the red light goes off; this indicates that the coffee is finished.

Figure 5-7. *(continued)*

9. At this time you may slide the filter holder off the machine, remove the filter, replace it with an unused filter, and repeat the process for another pot of coffee.

To make tea, follow the same process, only do not put the filter and coffee in the filter holder.

INHILCO TRAINING

HOW TO MAKE COFFEE IN THE CORY COFFEE MAKER	POSITION Server	DATE 2/9/78
	DEPARTMENT Rotisserie	PAGE 17

During slow periods, wait until one pot of coffee is almost empty before making the next one. This is to keep the coffee fresh.

Before peak volume periods, pre-prepare several filters with coffee and let them stand in a dry area. This will facilitate making coffee when you are busy. During busy periods, make coffee as often as necessary to keep up with the volume.

employee, or an outside consultant you hire for this purpose. You may have good writers on your staff who can write the manual for you. For example, a waiter may be quite capable of writing the server, busser, and host manuals. He should be paid equitably for his efforts, above his hourly rate when he works as a server. The manual may also be written as a joint effort among several people. This has the advantage of spreading the job around and expediting the writing; however, it can turn out to be nonhomogeneous if the writers have very different styles. If more than one writer is used, decide in advance on the format and style of the manual so there will be uniformity in the product.

Set a Deadline and Stick to It

Make the writing of the manual a priority and not something that should be done when there is time. (There is never time.) The deadline should be

Figure 5-8. Lunch setup of bain marie. (Courtesy of Inhilco, Inc.)

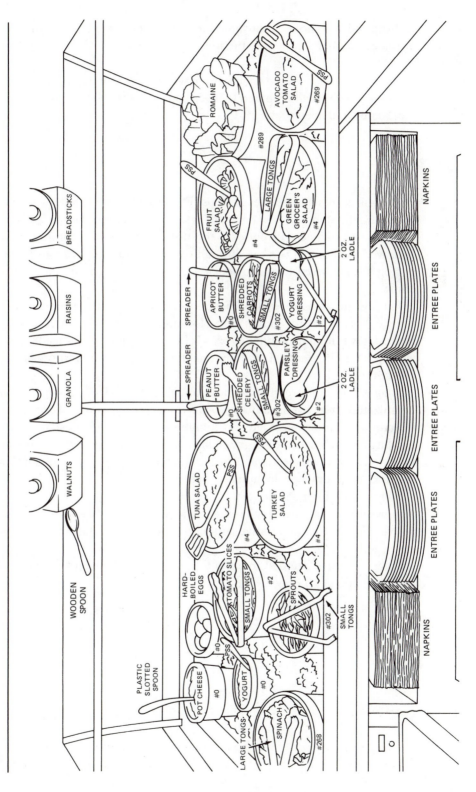

realistic and you should allow time for writing in the writer's schedule so he or she can actually complete the job on time.

Once you have analyzed each job and written the training manual for each position, you are well prepared to teach someone the jobs in your restaurant thoroughly and accurately.

SUMMARY

Every task consists of a series of steps. The task indicates what the trainee is to do, and the steps tell how he or she is to do it. It is important to specify the steps so the trainee will perform the tasks of the job according to your approved methods. It is often difficult to identify the steps of a task once a person has mastered them, so specifying the steps often takes a conscious effort.

Putting the steps in writing benefits the operator, the trainer, and the trainee. When the procedures for performing a job's tasks are put in writing, the result is a training manual. Clarity is the most important consideration in writing a training manual; the material must be clear in both organization and content.

Suggestions for organizing the manual are: (1) Decide on the basic organization, which is usually by job position; (2) have a table of contents; (3) include a welcome message; (4) number the pages; (5) design a special heading for the pages; (6) begin each task on a new page; (7) subdivide the material; (8) give credit to the trainers who helped prepare the material; and (9) have the manual professionally typed.

Suggestions for presenting the content are: (1) Explain each task in a step-by-step manner using full sentences; (2) use simple language; (3) use the active voice and use imperative sentences; and (4) use pictures to clarify your message.

Once you have decided to write a training manual, select a writer, set a deadline, and get it done!

PART FOUR

TRAINERS

6

Selecting, Developing, and Rewarding Trainers

In all but the smallest operations, the manager cannot handle employee training alone. There is a need to delegate many aspects of training to supervisors and to trusted hourly employees, while maintaining overall control. For example, if a new dishwasher were hired, you, the manager, would not be likely to personally handle all aspects of his training. You might give the new hire his orientation, then the employee's immediate supervisor, with the aid of an hourly employee, would normally do the skills training. So, the problem of training employees becomes more complex than just, "How shall I train my employees?" It becomes, "How shall I train my trainers to train my employees?" You must accomplish a great deal through the performance of your staff, and training, too, must be accomplished with the aid of the staff.

Who Can Assist with Training?

Before discussing how hourly employees, the peers of the trainees, can assist you in training new employees, let us identify in more general terms the people who can assist with training. When using any of these training resources, you need to clearly communicate the points you would like the instructor to make, so the lessons are as helpful as possible to you and your staff.

Suppliers

Suppliers will often assist their customers by conducting training related to their products. In many cases, the supplier will conduct training classes with audiovisual training programs, handouts, and other materials to make an interesting and informative presentation.

Wine suppliers are frequently used. Some will provide "dummy" bottles (empty, capped bottles) for the staff to practice opening the wine. Often they will provide prizes for incentive programs, such as sweaters, wine buckets, and bottles of wine. Direct the suppliers to cover the general information needed by the staff and not to focus exclusively on their products. Some topics wine suppliers can address are the history of wine, the fermentation process, the systems for naming wine, the characteristics of wine, the characteristics of the different grapes, an analysis of the restaurant's wine list, the making of appropriate wine suggestions, the blending of food and wine, and the proper way to open and serve wine at the table. You might even get the supplier's permission to tape-record these seminars and use the tapes to train new employees. You may also want to prepare a handout and quiz based on the instructor's material.

Suppliers of soda will instruct the staff on filling, cleaning, and using the soda dispensers. Detergent suppliers have programs on sanitation, operating the dish machine, pot washing, and other cleaning chores. Shortening suppliers have programs on frying and griddling foods. Check with your suppliers on the training programs they offer.

Red Cross/Paramedics

All restaurant managers should know how to aid a choking victim. The technique involves removing a foreign body from obstructing the airway. The local Red Cross or paramedics usually teach this technique at a very reasonable cost. You may want all your key personnel to have this training. Many restaurant operators have saved people's lives by knowing how to dislodge the obstructing object when a person is choking. Other courses the Red Cross and paramedics can teach include first aid and CPR.

The Board of Health

The local public health authorities may be willing to instruct on sanitation. Using the health inspectors may also impress them with your efforts to train your staff in proper sanitation techniques. Topics should include food-borne illnesses and how they are caused, the conditions necessary for germs to grow, personal hygiene, food handling, and cleaning.

The State Restaurant Association

Your state restaurant association may offer training programs to members in topics such as the responsible service of alcohol and customer service techniques. Many associations have libraries of commercially available video training programs, as well as books on service, cooking, and other topics that can aid in training. It may be worthwhile joining your state association for its educational resources as well as its other benefits to members.

The National Restaurant Association

The National Restaurant Association offers educational seminars in most major cities around the country, as well as videotapes and handbooks. For information on its educational programs, contact the NRA's Washington, D.C. office through its toll-free number.

The Police

The local police department may be helpful in instructing employees on how to avoid a robbery and what to do in case of a robbery. The police may also be called on for instruction on how to handle the intoxicated guest.

The Fire Department

The local fire department can be helpful in training for fire safety and for evacuation of the restaurant in an emergency. Firefighters can show the staff how to operate the fire extinguishers and perhaps explain some of the other fire safety equipment as well.

Schools

Colleges in the area may have programs in foodservice, business, or film production. Sometimes restaurants have gotten students to write training manuals or to produce audiovisual programs as term projects. It would be worth investigating the local school programs to determine if preparing training materials for your restaurant may be considered as part of a course's requirements.

Using Peers as Trainers

Peers, or hourly employees doing the same or similar jobs, are often used to train new employees. As previously discussed, in order for this system to have merit, it must be carefully structured and closely supervised. Care must be taken in selecting, developing, and rewarding trainers.

Selecting Trainers
Attitude

Trainers should have the kind of attitude you would like your new employees to acquire toward the job. This attitude involves a combination of serious-ness and enthusiasm.

Trainers should take their own job seriously and project its importance to the trainee. The following example indicates the kind of seriousness that you would want a trainer to have and to communicate to the trainee about sanitation: "You need to be sure the counters are cleaned and wiped thoroughly. It's important because we don't want any germs to grow and we don't want any pests attracted by the dirty counters. We have a responsibility to our guests to maintain the most sanitary conditions possible."

Trainers should also be enthusiastic about their jobs. They should project to the new employees that the work is fun.

Finally, the trainers should hold you, the manager, in esteem. They should respect you so that they will speak well of you to the trainees.

Competence

Trainers should be competent workers, who will serve as good role models. They should be conscientious and meticulous about details, because the trainees will be watching and emulating them. Because their behavior can have a profound and lasting influence on the people they train, the trainers must know and do their jobs well.

Teaching Skills

It is not enough to be competent at the job. Not every good tennis player would make a good tennis instructor. The trainer must also have or be capable of acquiring good teaching skills. The important attributes of a good teacher include clearly articulating what one is doing, demonstrating tasks slowly and in an organized manner, repeating information patiently, being tolerant of a newcomer's mistakes, testing the trainee to be sure he or she knows in detail how to perform each task, putting the trainee at ease, and encouraging questions.

A Volunteer

Sometimes you may find a volunteer to be the trainer. This person may enjoy teaching others. Perhaps it is someone who has raised children or taught school. If the person you select as trainer actually wants the job, the results will probably be better than with a trainer who feels forced into that position.

How Many Trainers?

How many trainers do you need? It depends. In a simple operation, perhaps one for the front and another for the back of the house. The trainer should be able to work any position for which he or she trains someone. For example, a front-of-the-house trainer who is to train people for host, server, and busser positions should be able to work these positions. The trainer may normally work as a server, but can be scheduled as a busser or host when training a person for one of those positions. (Of course, if you ask a server to work as a busser or host, compensation should be made for lost tips.)

Developing Trainers

Trainers' skills need to be developed. They need to be shown the effective way to teach someone a job, which is explained in Chapter 7. In a large operation, it may be worthwhile to develop a formal course for training trainers, as is done by some hotel and restaurant companies. Hourly employees chosen as trainers are given a course, usually lasting one or two days, in which they are trained to be trainers. They are familiarized with the training manuals and other materials used, and they get an opportunity to teach tasks to others in the course. They may even be videotaped as they give instruction, with the video segment played back and constructively critiqued by the class.

Refer to Figures 6-1 through 6-14 for exercises used in a train-the-trainer course. The exercises are based on the skills training method that is outlined in Chapter 7 on individualized instruction.

If the operation is small and a formal training program for trainers is not practical, the training must be done informally. You need to explain to your trainers what you want them to teach and how to teach it. It would be helpful to make a game out of the trainers' teaching you the tasks so you can check on the content and delivery of the lessons. For example, have a kitchen trainer explain to you how to operate the dish machine.

A very important way of controlling the content of the instruction is to furnish the trainer with materials for training. These materials should include (1) the job checklist, indicating the tasks needed to teach the new person; (2) the training manual, indicating how each task is to be performed; (3) any audiovisual programs the trainee is to view as part of the training; (4) the training schedule (which will be discussed later); and (5) quizzes and performance evaluations the trainer is to use to assess the trainee's performance. Furnishing the trainer with these tools for training will enable you to control the instruction.

The training materials are your procedures and guidelines which are communicated to the trainee through the trainer. This is how it has to be.

Explanation of Figures 6-1 Through 6-14

Figures 6-1 through 6-14 are exercises from a two-day train-the-trainer course given for rank-and-file employees. The purpose of the course was to teach these employees how to give individualized instruction to new employees. The workbooks of the participants had many exercises, such as the ones shown in the following pages, to teach someone a skill using the method described in Chapter 7. You may want to review these exercises after reading that chapter, which will help clarify this material.

The exercises are "programmed instructional." A flap in the notebook covered the left side of the page while the students worked on the exercises on the right side. Then the students checked their answers with those given on the left side. Audiocassette exercises were also used in the program.

The first day of the course, the students were given homework. They were to prepare to teach an assigned task to someone else in the class. Tasks included how to mop a floor, how to clean the slicer, how to take an order, etc., depending on their particular jobs. They had to bring all necessary props with them and conduct their lessons for the class. The lessons were videotaped and played back for the students. Praise and constructive suggestions for improvement were given to each student. The discussion was led by the instructor with class participation. The critique was done in a straightforward yet friendly manner, so the students learned from the experience without being offended by the criticism.

These classes were held at Inhilco, Inc., and all exercises are reproduced here with Inhilco's permission.

(Text continued on p. 100)

Figure 6-1. Breaking a job into tasks. (Courtesy of Inhilco, Inc.)

In front of each task listed on the right, write in the name of the job on the left that the task belongs to:

JOB	TASK

Dishwasher—
scrape plates at dish machine

Cook—
make scrambled eggs

Dishwasher—
sort silverware after cleaning

Server—
serve wine

Cashier—
place cash in register drawer

Dishwasher—
put detergent in machine

Cashier—
count change

Cook—
broil meats

Server—
serve coffee

Server _____ Scrape plates at dish machine

Cook _____ Make scrambled eggs

Dishwasher _____ Sort silverware after cleaning

Cashier _____ Serve wine

_____ Place cash in register drawer

_____ Put detergent in machine

_____ Count change

_____ Broil meats

_____ Serve coffee

Figure 6-2. Breaking a job into tasks. (Courtesy of Inhilco, Inc.)

_____

Place a J next to the job, a T next to the task, and an S next to the steps in that task:

__S__   _____ Turn on grill to 350 degrees

__S__   _____ Get cutting board from shelf and place on work counter

__T__   _____ Set up station in the morning

__S__   _____ Remove 5 dozen eggs from walk-in refrigerator and place on counter

__J__   _____ Breakfast cook

__S__   _____ Place mop in bucket of cleaning solution

__J__   _____ Kitchen cleaner

__S__   _____ Pass mop through wringer to remove excess water

__T__   _____ Mop a floor

__S__   _____ Be sure floor has been swept before you begin

Figure 6-3. Breaking a task into steps. (Courtesy of Inhilco, Inc.)

Some tasks which a coffee shop waitress would have to do are:

1. Order and pick up food
2. Set tables and counters
3. Set up station in the morning
4. Suggest items to the guests

Indicate the number of the task above which each of the following steps belongs to:

___3___ _____ The first thing in the morning, turn on bun warmer

___1___ _____ Pick up ice cream orders at ice cream window

___3___ _____ Fill 3 cake stands with breakfast pastry and place on your station

___4___ _____ Watch for empty glasses so you can suggest refills on beverages

___2___ _____ Place knife, fork, and spoon on top of the napkin

___2___ _____ Place salt, pepper, and sugar bowl on every table

___4___ _____ Whenever guest orders a hamburger, ask if he would also like french fries

___1___ _____ Place order on spindle for the cook to read

Figure 6-4. Breaking a task into steps. (Courtesy of Inhilco, Inc.)

We would teach someone the steps in the order in which they would have to be done.

Number the following steps in the order in which you would teach them. (Two answers have been given)

TASK: HOW TO MAKE COFFEE

STEPS:

__3__   _____Empty 2 bags of coffee into the filter

__5__   ___5___Cover urn

__1__   ___1___Be sure urn and basket are clean

__4__   _____Place filled basket on top of urn

__2__   _____Place a large filter firmly in the basket

__6__   _____Press button marked BREW to make coffee

Figure 6-5. Preparing to teach. (Courtesy of Inhilco, Inc.)

Check the statements by you which will make your trainee feel comfortable and relaxed:

_____✓_____ "These things take time. Try it again. I'm sure you'll get the hang of it."

_____✓_____ "Yes, turn the hamburger using the spatula."

_____✓_____ "That was excellent. Now try the next step."

_____✓_____ "A cocktail tray should never be placed on the table. Balance the tray in one hand and serve with the other hand."

_____ "Try to do it right this time, I don't have all day."

_____ "These things take time. Try it again. I'm sure you'll get the hang of it."

_____ "Of course you have to turn the hamburger. Did you think you just cooked it on one side?"

_____ "Yes, turn the hamburger using the spatula."

_____ "That was excellent. Now try the next step."

_____ "Stop! Don't put that cocktail tray on the table. This isn't the YMCA!"

_____ "A cocktail tray should never be placed on the table. Balance the tray in one hand and serve with the other hand."

Figure 6-6. Preparing to teach. (Courtesy of Inhilco, Inc.)

task

Before you are ready to teach you must know what task you are teaching and what steps are necessary to do that _____.

Indicate which attitudes·on your part are helpful to your trainee:

___✓___ encouragement

___✓___ confidence

___✓___ willingness to answer questions

___✓___ willingness to praise
materials

_____ impatience
_____ encouragement
_____ intolerance of mistakes
_____ confidence
_____ hostility
_____ willingness to answer questions
_____ willingness to praise

Gather the necessary _____ before you begin the lesson.

Figure 6-7. Introducing the lesson. (Courtesy of Inhilco, Inc.)

Introduce the lesson by telling the trainee:

1. What he will learn.

1. _____
   _____

2. Why he needs to learn it.

2. _____
   _____

In the following introduction, circle the part that tells the trainee what he is going to learn, and underline the part that tells him why he needs to learn it.

"Today you will learn how to use the deep fat fryer. Using the fryer correctly will enable you to turn out a high-quality french fry. About 25% of your customers order fries, so you will be using the fryer often.
[In this case 2 reasons were given.]

"Today you will learn how to use the deep fat fryer. Using the fryer correctly will enable you to turn out a high-quality french fry. About 25% of your customers order fries, so you will be using the fryer often.

"Today you will learn how to check coats and bags. It is very important to do this properly to assure that the guest can retrieve his belongings without any problem at the end of the meal."

"Today you will learn how to check coats and bags. It is very important to do this properly to assure that the guest can retrieve his belongings without any problem at the end of the meal."

"In order to avoid your slicing your fingers, I want to show you the proper way to use the slicer."

"In order to avoid your slicing your fingers, I want to show you the proper way to use the slicer."

Figure 6-8. Teaching the task. (Courtesy of Inhilco, Inc.)

Your explanations should be clear and precise and they should cover only 1 step at a time.

For the following explanations, indicate one of the following:

1. Needs to give more information
2. Covers more than one step
3. Is good as written

___1___   _____ "Pour egg mix on the griddle."

___3___   _____ "Pour one 3-oz. ladle of egg mix on the portion of the griddle you just greased."

___2___   _____ "Pour egg mix on griddle and turn eggs over as soon as they start getting firm."

___2___   _____ "Answer the phone, and find out the day, date, and time of the reservation desired."

___1___   _____ "Answer the phone."

___3___   _____ "Answer the phone by saying, 'Good afternoon, Reservations, may I help you?'"

Figure 6-9. Teaching the task. (Courtesy of Inhilco, Inc.)

It is important that you demonstrate the step before you have the trainee practice it. This allows the trainee to see the step done correctly before he tries it.

Which procedure is correct in teaching the step to a trainee?

_____ "Rub the stone on the griddle with me."

___✓___ "First, watch me rub the stone on the griddle. Then you can try it."

_____ "First, watch me rub the stone on the griddle. Then you can try it."

Figure 6-10. Teaching the task. (Courtesy of Inhilco, Inc.)

Reword the following explanations to include teaching questions.

Example:
"The portion size is half a chicken, so cut the chicken in half lengthwise."

"The portion size is half a chicken. How do you think we should cut it, lengthwise or widthwise?"

Note: other correct answers are possible.

"When you approach the table for the first time, greet the guests."

"What's the first thing you should do when you approach the table for the first time?"

"_____
_____
_____
_____."

"Do not press the hamburger down with the spatula while cooking it."

"Why should you not press the hamburger down with the spatula while cooking it?"

"_____
_____
_____
_____."

"Place the cup on the guest's tray by holding it at the base, not the rim."

"Place the cup on the guest's tray. How should you hold it?"

"_____
_____
_____."

Figure 6-11. Testing the trainee. (Courtesy of Inhilco, Inc.)

---

3 PARTS TO A LESSON:

1. INTRODUCTION

Teaching section   2. _____

Testing section   3. _____

step

In the teaching section you teach the trainee how to perform each _____ in the task.

In the testing section you have the trainee show you that he can do the _____ by himself.

entire task

In the teaching section you demonstrate each step.

In the testing section you do not demonstrate the steps, but ask the trainee to do the task by himself.

Figure 6-12. Testing the trainee. (Courtesy of Inhilco, Inc.)

In the teaching section the trainee gets practice:

_____✓_____ doing each step in the task after you demonstrate it

_____ doing each step in the task after you demonstrate it

_____ doing the entire task by himself

In the testing section, the trainee gets practice:

_____ doing each step in the task after you demonstrate it

_____✓_____ doing the entire task by himself

_____ doing the entire task by himself

Figure 6-13. Testing the trainee. (Courtesy of Inhilco, Inc.)

In the testing section you:

_____ explain each step to the trainee

_____✓_____ ask testing questions

_____ ask testing questions

_____ demonstrate each step to the trainee

_____✓_____ have the trainee do the entire task himself

_____ have the trainee do the entire task himself

Figure 6-14. Testing the trainee. (Courtesy of Inhilco, Inc.)

Suppose you have just taught a server how to make a ham and cheese sandwich; what kinds of testing questions might you ask?

E.g.
"If a customer wants lettuce and tomato, in what order would you add the meat, cheese, lettuce, and tomato to the sandwich?"

"Tell me, from beginning to end, what steps you would do to make this sandwich."

(This last question is an excellent way for the trainee to review the entire task.)

(Many correct answers are possible)
"What types of bread do you have to offer the customer?"

Do you cut the sandwich in half? Diagonally or down the center?"

"How would you find out if the customer wants a dressing on the sandwich, and how would you spread it on?"

Formulate 2 more testing questions:

Question 1: "_____
_____
_____"

Question 2: "_____
_____
_____"

Trainers should not be left to their own devices to teach the tasks they deem important in the manner in which they think the tasks should be performed. This information should come from you, and the trainers should be your means of communicating your standards to new hires. In order to accomplish this, the trainers must be thoroughly briefed on what your standards are and must have the tools to communicate your message.

Rewarding Trainers

Too often the position of trainer is one that no one wants. Employees feel imposed upon when they are asked not only to perform their jobs but to train others as well. A supervisor can be asked to train employees and simply told that it is part of the job. Training is part of management and supervision; however, it is not part of a server's, busser's, cook's, or other nonsupervisory job. If you ask a rank-and-file employee to be a trainer, it is important to reward that person's efforts. Rewarding the trainer indicates your recognition of the fact that he or she is doing something extra for you, above and beyond the job's requirements. It also shows your appreciation for the trainer's assistance. Compensation is necessary to motivate employees to be trainers and to perform the training well.

Below are some ways in which foodservice companies have rewarded their trainers.

Pay Increase

Some trainers are given a pay increase. This may be an across-the-board increase in hourly wage, or it may be an increase only for the hours spent training. For example, a cook may earn an extra $.50 an hour for the time he spends training another employee. The across-the-board increase is usually given when the trainer spends a great deal of time training employees or when the trainer also takes on other responsibilities. For example, a waitress may be paid more per hour than the other servers if she trains servers and bussers and does the scheduling as well.

Bonus

Sometimes the trainer is given a bonus for producing a properly trained employee. The bonus might be anywhere from $25 to $100, depending on the operation and on the amount of work required of the trainer. This bonus might be split, with half given immediately after the trainee is trained and the other half given after three months, provided the trainee has remained with the company and is still doing a good job. This kind of reward gives the trainer a vested interest in following up with the trainee after the initial training to be sure the newcomer is happy with the job and performing well.

Special Privileges

The trainer may be given first preferences in schedule, vacation, or stations. The trainer may get an upgraded employee meal. For example, if the policy is to discount employee meals, the trainer may get a free meal. Or, if the policy is to limit selections from the menu for the staff meal, the trainer may be given more choices. Hotels with health club facilities may offer the trainer the use of those facilities. Lift tickets may be offered to trainers at ski resorts. Tickets to sports events or concerts are also attractive rewards. Some trainers are given gift certificates for complimentary meals at the restaurant or at another restaurant in the company. One company gives its trainers up to $50 per month in complimentary meal privileges in its restaurants.

Trainers may also be asked to report on the food, service, and atmosphere while enjoying their complimentary meal. Or they may be given the opportunity to shop the competition, in which case they get a complimentary meal for two in exchange for a report on their dining experience at a competitor's restaurant. These kinds of rewards offer the restaurant valuable information and serve as further training for the trainers.

Advancement

If there is opportunity for advancement within your company, trainers can be given first consideration for supervisory positions. This reward has worked extremely well for organizations large enough to have frequent supervisory openings. The job of trainer then becomes an intermediate position for rank-and-file employees you are priming for advancement. If you have a small company without opportunities for advancement, a fair trade may be your willingness to teach the trainer how to run a business in exchange for training your employees. This may involve your spending some time explaining how to get a business off the ground, which could be of great interest to someone who aspires to owning a restaurant or other business in the future.

Educational Opportunities

Trainers can be given the opportunity to attend National Restaurant Association seminars when they are given locally. You may also offer partial tuition reimbursement for courses taken at a local college. This is a benefit to career-minded employees desiring to improve themselves.

Recognition

Some companies will bestow their trainers with a pin or other mark of distinction, usually to be worn on the uniform. This distinguishes the trainers from the other employees. Marks of distinction serve to alert guests, too, to the trainers' achievements. Recognition in the form of pins, praise, or other demonstrations of your appreciation is important, because trainers need to be thanked for their efforts. However, recognition should be used in combination with other awards that have actual material value, so your trainers do not feel that you are merely offering them a pat on the back and a pin. They may justifiably feel they deserve more than a few kind words for their efforts.

Trainers are an essential part of any training program. Their selection, development, and compensation should be carefully considered in designing your training program.

SUMMARY

The manager needs to delegate training to others. Who can assist with training? Suppliers, the Red Cross, the board of health, state restaurant associations, the National Restaurant Association, the police and fire departments, and local schools may be able to assist with certain aspects of employee training.

Rank-and-file employees can be most helpful in training others who do the same or similar jobs. In selecting trainers from the ranks of employees, their attitude, competence, and teaching ability are important considerations. It is advisable to try a volunteer if there is an employee who wants to be a trainer.

The trainer's skill needs to be developed. In large companies a formal train-the-trainer course should be given to prepare employees for their role as trainers. In a smaller organization, the manager needs to informally guide the trainer. An important way of controlling the training is to provide the trainer with the necessary tools to do the job according to the operation's standards. These tools include the job checklist, the training manual, audiovisual aids, the training schedule, and quizzes and performance evaluations.

Trainers should be rewarded for their efforts. Rewards for trainers may include a pay increase, a bonus, special privileges, advancement opportunities, educational opportunities, and recognition.

Trainers are an important part of any training program. Their selection, development, and compensation should be carefully considered.

PART FIVE

TEACHING SKILLS

7

Individualized Instruction

In the preceding chapters we have discussed how to break a job down into tasks and how to break the tasks down into steps. This analysis of the job answers the question, "What do you want to teach?" We also discussed selecting, developing, and rewarding trainers in answer to the question, "Who will do the teaching?" Now we are ready to answer the next question in our sequence, "How will you train?" Once the details and requirements of the job are identified, you are ready to communicate that information to the trainee. In this and the next two chapters, methods are described for giving individualized instruction and group instruction, and for using audiovisuals in training. First, let us consider individualized instruction.

Individualized instruction is given by a trainer to one trainee. (If instead there are two or three trainees, the trainer is usually able to give what amounts to individualized instruction.) Occasions for individualized instruction are the hiring of a new employee or the change of position of an employee, such as a dishwasher being promoted to a cook. The purpose of this instruction is to teach a particular job to someone new to the position. This kind of one-on-one training is an excellent way to learn a job, just as private tennis lessons are usually more effective than group lessons. The attention devoted to the trainee in individualized instruction cannot be matched in a group setting. The teaching is more specialized and the learning is more rapid.

The following are guidelines for training individuals. These are the kinds of skills that you and/or your trainers need to master to do a good job of training.

Respect the Trainee

The trainer must work to build mutual respect with the trainee. A show of respect for the trainee will earn the trainee's respect in return. Some of the ways in which the trainer can show respect for the trainee are (1) being tolerant of mistakes and not making the trainee feel inadequate for errors, (2) having confidence in the trainee's ability to master a task, and (3) treating the trainee's questions seriously and not laughing at them no matter how naive or silly they may sound. The trainer's respectful attitude will place the trainee at ease so the latter can learn most effectively. It will also build respect in the trainee for the trainer, the job, and the company.

Teach Tasks One at a Time

The job must be clearly explained to the trainee. As discussed previously, this requires that the job be broken down into a series of tasks and the tasks into steps. Learning is only possible when the trainee is not overwhelmed and confused by a hodgepodge of random, unintegrated data. The learning needs to be organized, and it is the job breakdown that organizes it.

In the actual performance of the job, tasks will often overlap. For example, a cook may get orders for a hamburger, french fries, and an omelet at the same time. He will not prepare each item one at a time, but will work on all three orders simultaneously. This is as it should be when the cook has mastered the tasks and is performing his job. However, this kind of overlapping of tasks is not the best way to teach the job. It is confusing. Contrary to the way they are performed on the job once they are mastered, tasks should be taught separately. The new cook should be taught from beginning to end how to make the burger, the omelet, and the fries as separate tasks.

The separation of tasks is important in making the job clear. Presenting one whole task from beginning to end allows the trainee to integrate the steps mentally and grasp the whole task. Whenever possible, the trainer should teach one task at a time.

Separating the tasks for teaching is also one of the most difficult problems for the restaurant operator. On-the-job training is practical, yet on the job the tasks overlap. Separating the tasks requires that the training be done during slow periods or that the on-the-job training be supplemented with some off-the-job training sessions in which one task at a time can be taught. (We'll discuss this point in greater detail in the section on developing a training schedule.)

Some managers like to throw new employees into the heat of action immediately to see how tough they are, on the premise that employees who can survive that kind of abuse during their training period can survive anything. While it is desirable to be demanding of one's employees, a manager has a right to be demanding only after the employee is properly trained. Employees who have previous experience or those who are highly motivated may survive a "baptism by fire," but more often such abuse will cause stress and lead to the turnover of those who could otherwise have become good employees. Even those who survive improper training often do not know the job as well as they would have if they were properly trained.

Separating the tasks also limits the subject matter taught at any one time. For example, if one were teaching someone how to prepare a chef's salad, one should not at the same time go off on tangents such as trying to explain how to make the salad dressings or how to deep fry the tortilla bowl in which the salad may be served. Learning is much easier when the subject matter of any one training session is limited to that which can be grasped at one sitting. So the tasks should be broken down enough to teach a task at one training session. The trainer should make an effort to refrain from covering related tasks until the trainee understands the intended subject of the session.

Explain, Demonstrate, and Practice

There is one method that is effective in teaching any type of skill. It can be used to teach a pilot how to fly a plane, a mechanic how to fix a car's engine, or a doctor how to remove an appendix. The method of teaching anyone a skill is essentially universal, and it consists of three key elements: explanation, demonstration, and practice.

Explanation
Explain Slowly and Articulately

The explanation should be slow and articulate. The trainer needs to speak slowly so the information can be understood and retained. When training is done during high-volume business, it obviously is not possible for the trainer to explain slowly, which often causes the trainee to become confused. The trainer also needs to be articulate, clearly expressing the ideas of the lesson and identifying the things to which he or she refers. For example, in explaining how to open wine, a good trainer will say something like, "Using the knife of the corkscrew, cut the cap below the lip of the bottle." A trainer who instead says, "Use this to cut that," is not being articulate, and this will make learning more difficult.

Give the Reasons

Another technique that makes the explanation clear is giving reasons. It is very illuminating to trainees to understand why they are asked to do things a certain way. It makes the trainees better able to retain the instruction if they understand the reasons for the policies and procedures they are taught. Consider the following examples:

• Setting the table: There is a logic to the way the table is set, and a trainee who understands the rules of place setting will be more likely to remember where everything goes. Explain to the trainee why forks are placed to the left and knives and spoons to the right, that is, because we always assume a right-handed universe. Explain why we always set the table with the first course's utensils on the outside, and why the knife blade faces the plate.

• Preparing a chef's salad: Explain why the salad should be served on a chilled plate, why the appearance of the salad is important, and why the correct portioning of ingredients is important. The trainee should clearly understand employee impact on the restaurant's costs. For example, if the trainee will be making approximately 20 chef's salads a day, 5 days a week, 50 weeks a year—a total of 5000 chef's salads a year—and if each were overportioned by one ounce of ham, the trainee should know how much money the restaurant would lose as a result of the incorrect portioning. Giving reasons helps the trainee understand the impact of his or her actions on the restaurant's profitability.

Ask the Trainee Questions

Another technique that makes explanations clear is asking the trainee questions. Asking questions serves several useful purposes: (1) It forces the trainee to think about the subject while being taught; (2) it reviews the subject in the trainee's mind after it has been taught; and (3) it allows the trainer to find out how much the trainee knows and to gear the lesson accordingly. Let's discuss each of these purposes in greater detail:

1. Forcing the Trainee to Think. If the trainer interjects the presentation with questions of the kind that cannot be answered "yes" or "no," the trainee is forced to speak and, therefore, forced to think. Questions that ask for information—such as *who, what, where, why, how, how many,* and *when*— will get the trainee to think. For example: "Why do you suppose we cap the soiled ashtray with the clean one?" "What would you use to turn the hamburger?" "How do you think we can avoid getting salt in the fry kettle?"

One can help the trainee to figure out the next steps in the task he or she is learning by such questions as, "Now that you have the party's order of salads and soups, which will you prepare first?"

The purpose of asking questions during the lesson is to keep the trainee's attention and to get him or her to think about the task being learned. Questions asked during the lesson are not meant to test or to discourage the trainee. Therefore, these questions should be ones the trainee will be likely to answer correctly. If the trainee does not know the answer, try an encouraging hint. For example, "What do you think we do now that the fries are cooked?" If the trainee replies that the fries should be removed from the fry basket and transferred to a pan, the trainer might say: "Well, since the grease is still dripping from the fries, what would you do before transferring the fries to the pan?" The answer the trainer seeks is that the trainee will allow the grease to drain from the fries for a few seconds over the kettle before transferring them to a pan.

2. Reviewing the Subject After the Lesson is Completed. Questions asked after a lesson has been taught will serve to review the lesson in the trainee's mind. This will greatly aid retention. These questions are meant to test the trainee for understanding of the lesson and to clarify any misconceptions. Review questions should encompass the entire lesson and particularly focus on points the trainer wants to emphasize. Here are some examples of review questions a trainer might ask after giving a lesson on how to prepare a chef's salad: "What ingredients would you use in the chef's salad?" "How many ounces of cheese, ham, and turkey would you place on the salad?" "Explain to me how you would make the salad." "How would you garnish the salad?" "What type of plate would you place the salad on?"

3. Allowing the Trainer to Find out How Much the Trainee Knows. Asking the proper questions is also an invaluable aid to the trainer to determine precisely what the trainee knows and does not know. "Do you understand?" is usually not a good question, because many trainees will be afraid to admit they do not understand. It is up to the trainer to find out whether the trainee understands or not, and this can be done very effectively through the use of skillful questions. When working with an employee who has prior experience, the trainer may want to ask a number of questions in advance of teaching a particular task to see if the trainee already knows how to do the task.

Demonstration

The second key element in teaching someone a skill is demonstration. The trainer must demonstrate how to perform the task correctly and, by doing so, should serve as a role model for the trainee to emulate. The combination of explanation and demonstration will give the trainee both the knowledge to perform as well as the model of someone performing correctly. Explanation and demonstration give the trainee *knowledge* of how to perform the task and *application* of that knowledge in performing the task.

The trainer should not wait until the end of an explanation of the entire task to begin the demonstration. He or she should explain one or a few steps, then demonstrate them. Often the explanation and demonstration will occur simultaneously. For example, consider the task of serving wine at the table. The trainer should demonstrate, while explaining how to present the wine to the person who ordered it, how to remove the cap from the bottle, then remove the cork, then pour a taste for the person who ordered the wine, etc.

Practice

The trainee needs to practice the task in order to master it. It is usually best if the trainer does not wait until the end of the entire task to ask the trainee to practice. If the task consists of 20 steps, the trainee will not be able to retain them. However, if the trainer stops after a few steps and has the trainee practice, the retention will be improved. For example, in serving wine at the table, the trainer might explain how to present the wine to the host, demonstrate this, then have the trainee practice it. Then the trainer would go on to explain how to remove the cap, demonstrate it, and have the trainee practice. The same steps would apply to removing the cork, and so on. This is how a well-structured lesson should run.

Trainer and trainee should not be doing things at the same time. First, the trainer should demonstrate the action. The trainee should be watching and not trying to practice at the same time. Then, the trainee should practice and the trainer should be observing. If the trainee practices at the same time the trainer demonstrates, neither can watch the other and the instruction will not be as effective.

This side-by-side demonstration and practice is sometimes impossible. For example, if the trainee must be taught how to broil steaks, you are not going to want steaks wasted in practice. Here, the training might take place on the job during a slow period. The trainer first broils a steak as the trainee watches. Then, as other orders come in, the trainee gets to practice. If carving a rack of lamb tableside must be taught, the operator is not going to be inclined to waste this product while the trainee practices carving. In this case the carving skills should be explained off the job, using a loaf of bread if necessary, for practice. The trainee should then watch the trainer carve lamb at tableside, until he or she is prepared to try it with reasonable success. The pre-preparation and understanding are important here.

For teaching skills that involve talking to the customer, the demonstration and practice take the form of role play. For example, in taking the order at the table, the trainer should take the trainee's order, then they should reverse roles and the trainee should take the trainer's order.

(Refer to Chapter 8 for role-play exercises used in training hostesses.)

Test the Trainee

Whenever possible, the training session should end with the trainee being able to perform the entire task correctly from beginning to end. If the lesson is on how to make a tuna sandwich, the trainee should be able to make the sandwich correctly at the end of the session.

If it is not possible on the spot, then sometime within the training period, the trainee should demonstrate to the trainer the ability to correctly perform each task on the checklist. For example, if the task involves setting up the cook's area, and if there is only one cook's area, the trainer should explain and demonstrate what to do, and in the next day or two, the trainee should practice with the trainer's guidance until he or she is able to set up the cook's line properly without supervision. When the trainee shows proficiency, the trainer should check off the task on the checklist.

Quizzes

A written quiz or quizzes should be prepared to test the trainee's knowledge of the job. (If the trainee cannot read or write English, give the quiz verbally.) A trainee who expects to be tested is more motivated to study the material carefully. Quizzes should be based on the information covered in the training program, so it should be easy to get a high grade if the trainee has paid attention. Quizzes are easiest to grade when they are short answer, consisting of multiple-choice, true-or-false, and fill-in-the-blank types of questions. If the trainee does not do well on the quiz, the trainer should review and explain the correct answers and the trainee should have an opportunity to take the quiz again. (If everything asked for on the quiz is important to the correct performance of the job, consider making 100% the passing grade.) New employees should not be punished for getting a low score, but rather the information they lack or have grasped incorrectly should be pointed out and they should be given a chance to retake the quiz and get a high grade. Refer to the dishwasher's quiz and the answer key in Figures 7-1 and 7-2, respectively.

Figure 7-1. Dishwasher quiz. (Courtesy of Mr. Steak, Inc.)

---

1. What is a dishwasher's main responsibility?

2. When emptying the bus tub, where are paper and bones disposed of? Where are food scraps disposed of?

3. Where do you put glasses when emptying the bus tub?

4. What are the minimum wash cycle and rinse cycle temperatures for a high-temperature dishwasher?

5. What are the minimum wash cycle and rinse cycle temperatures for a low-temperature dishwasher?

6. What is the procedure for sorting silverware before it is washed?

7. How do you transfer the *dry* silverware from one cone to another?

8. What are the four types of racks used by the dishwasher?

9. Why do we prerinse dishes before putting them in the dish machine?

10. How long should the disposal run each time?

11. If dirt or food is caked or hardened on the dishes, what is used to remove it?

12. What are the seven steps for emptying a bus tub?

13. Where do you put full racks of clean cups and glasses?

14. What are the last items to be washed in the evening?

15. What are the closing procedures for cleaning a dish machine?

16. List three things you would check for if you were having trouble with glasses spotting.

Figure 7-2. Dishwasher quiz answer key. (Courtesy of Mr. Steak, Inc.)

---

1. To supply the restaurant with clean glasses, silverware, and china.

2. Waste barrel; garbage disposal.

3. In the correct size glass rack.

4. The minimum for the wash cycle temperature is 150 degrees F. The minimum for the rinse cycle temperature is 180 degrees F.

5. The minimum for the wash and rinse cycle temperatures for a low-temperature machine is 140 degrees F.

6. Loosely sort eating ends down into cones and immerse into presoaking solution. When sufficiently soaked, invert into another cone eating ends up.

7. Eating ends down.

8. Flat rack, cup rack, plate rack, glass rack.

9. To loosen dried on food particles and remove most scraps.

10. 30 seconds each time.

11. A scrub pad.

12. Remove paper and put in trash can.
Remove silver and put in presoak solution.
Remove glasses and put in glass rack.
Remove plates and put in plate rack.
Remove cups and put in cup rack.
Put remaining food scraps in trash.
Rinse the bus tub and stack.

13. On the glassware cart.

14. The hood filters.

15. Turn off the tank heating element.
Turn off the booster heating element.
Open the drain valve.
Remove the interior screen traps and spray.
Close the doors.
Turn on the fill valve with the drain valve opened for approximately 20 seconds.
Turn off the fill valve.
Replace the interior screen traps.
Close the drain valve.
Turn on the fill valve to fill tank $1/3$ full.
Turn off the fill valve.

16. Check the wash and rinse temperatures on the dish machine.
Check the dish machine screens for obstruction.
Check the wash arms for freedom of movement and lack of obstruction.
Check the level and flow of rinse additive.
Check cleanliness of water in dish machine.
Check the soap dispenser for level and flow.

Testing Performance

Quizzes are important in testing trainees' knowledge and in motivating them to learn the details of the job; however, a high score on a quiz does not guarantee that a trainee's performance will be equally excellent. The trainee's overall performance needs to be evaluated at the end of the training program and periodically thereafter. The job checklist should be used as a performance evaluation, as well as a training tool. (Refer to the sample job checklists given in Chapter 4.)

Design the Training Schedule

The training schedule is the plan, or blueprint, for the training program. It indicates the stations at which the trainee will work, what he or she will learn, and when the training will take place. The schedule may last anywhere from one or two days to a few weeks, depending on the complexity of the job and the amount of training required.

Appreciate the Value of Having a Training Schedule

The training schedule is the operator's means of managing trainees' first few days (or weeks) on the job. The training schedule helps you control the instruction. The trainer cannot teach whatever he or she wants to, but is instructed to teach according to the schedule. The schedule is also very helpful to trainees because it lets them know what to expect and it decreases their stress to know that there is some systematic plan for learning the job.

Use the Job Checklist as a Guide in Developing the Training Schedule

The job checklist, discussed in Chapter 4, lists the training objectives. The list of tasks that comprise the job are what you are trying to teach the trainee. The training schedule should provide time for the trainee to learn each of the tasks on the job checklist.

Include Off-the-Job and On-the-Job Training

On-the-job training is done while the trainee and trainer are actually working, that is, waiting on customers, preparing food, or cleaning. Usually it is the trainer who is doing the job and the trainee who is following. (Although when the trainee begins to master the tasks, the two should switch places. Then the trainer can check off the tasks on the checklist as the trainee demonstrates competence in them by correctly teaching them to the trainer.) On-the-job training is obviously essential if the trainee is to learn the job. For some of the simpler jobs, most or all of the training may be accomplished on the job, especially if there are lull times during which the trainer will be able to explain tasks in detail to the trainee.

The problem with using on-the-job training exclusively is that the job has to take priority over the training. As a result, many compromises are often made. The trainee is used to fetch things, the trainer gets busy and has no time to explain the tasks, tasks overlap and are confusing, or the trainer leaves out information because it is impossible to concentrate on the demands of the job and the requirements of the trainee at the same time.

For these reasons it is often very desirable to include some off-the-job training time in the training schedule. Off-the-job training means instruction that is done when both the trainee and trainer are not on duty; that is, it is time in addition to the normal work shift which is spent exclusively for training. Off-the-job training may take the form of group meetings in which there is more than one trainee, or of individual lessons between one trainee and the trainer. It will usually take place at the work station, although it is different from on-the-job training. The difference is that off-the-job training is additional time allowed for the purpose of training, time in which the trainer is only occupied with training and not with performing the job.

Off-the-job training adds to the cost of training, because trainee and trainer have to be scheduled for additional hours; however, it has the advantage of the trainer's being able to explain things in greater detail. For example, consider the task of serving wine at the table. This task cannot be explained properly when the trainer is actually serving wine to guests. There are simply too many details and subtleties that the trainee will not pick up unless they are explicitly pointed out, and there is no way to point out these things at the table without neglecting the guests. Details such as where to cut the lead cap, how to hold the wine, how much to pour into the glass, and how to use the lever would not be readily noticed by a trainee who was simply watching the trainer serve wine to guests. This type of task must be taught off the job. (Ask your wine supplier for "dummy" bottles, i.e., capped empty bottles for the purpose of wine training.)

The on-the-job training can be combined with off-the-job sessions, as in the sample schedule for training servers given in Figure 7-3, to assure that all the details of each task are properly covered.

Train from the Simple to the Complex

If possible, start with simpler tasks and work the trainee up to the more complex tasks. One restaurant, for example, starts all new servers with

Figure 7-3. Training schedule for new servers.

ON-THE-JOB WORK SCHEDULE OF NEW SERVERS—
THE FIRST EIGHT SHIFTS

Shift	Assignment	Learning Objectives
1	Orientation	Become familiar with general policies and procedures.
	Trail hostess	Gain knowledge of station and table numbers, greeting and seating guests, hospitality in the dining room.
2	Trail busser	Learn where supplies are kept, location and stocking of wait stations, clearing and cleaning tables, setting tables, filling and carrying bus trays, serving coffee, serving bread, changing ashtrays, pouring water.
3, 4, 5	Trail server-trainer	Get practical service experience in all aspects of the server's job.
6, 7, 8	Small station	Trainee gets a small station and continues to be watched by trainer. When the trainee is ready for it, he gets a larger station.

OFF-THE-JOB TRAINING—MEETINGS WITH TRAINER

Trainer and trainee meet for 30 minutes after their shift each day until all the following lessons have been taught and the trainee has gotten a score of 90% or higher on each of the quizzes. The trainee is to read the relevant procedures in the manual before the trainer teaches them and to study them for the quizzes.

The topics listed below are taken from the server's job checklist. The trainer should elaborate on those tasks and subjects that are not easily graspable during the on-the-job training. The trainer should check off each task on the checklist when it is mastered by the trainee. The following schedule may be altered as necessary based on the trainee's progress.

Day	Lessons (Refer to the job checklist for specific tasks to be covered under each category.)
1	Opening duties and side work.
2, 3, 4	Service procedures.
5	Clearing and resetting the table.

6	Handling guest checks.
7	Quiz on service.
8, 9, 10	Product knowledge and tastings—the menu. Appetizers, soups, salads, entrees and desserts.
11	Quiz on the menu.
12, 13	Product knowledge and tastings—wine.
14, 15	Product knowledge and tastings—cocktails.
16	Suggestive selling techniques.
17	Quiz on cocktails and wine.
18	Overall evaluation of trainee's performance.

weekend buffet service. This way the server is learning how to take cocktail and dessert orders and does not at this point also have to master the weekday menu and take food orders. After a weekend with the buffet, most servers feel more experienced and competent when it comes time to learn the weekday lunch and/or dinner menus.

Some restaurants will start a server off as a host or hostess for a shift or two. This position is less complex, yet still gives the server knowledge of greeting guests, table and station numbers, and seating.

Include Cross-training

Cross-training is instructing employees to perform jobs other than their own. For example, dishwashers and bussers are frequently cross-trained so they can fill in for each other when necessary. Other reasons for cross-training include (1) preparing employees for advancement, such as cross-training bussers to be waiters; (2) acquainting persons with positions they have to supervise, such as cross-training a broiler cook, who is the head cook of the kitchen, for the fry cook's position; and (3) familiarizing employees with their co-workers' positions to promote understanding of each others' jobs, such as having servers work with cooks or vice versa for a shift or two to promote teamwork.

Cross-training can be important in the initial job training. For example, a server may briefly trail a host and a busser. The other jobs directly relate to the server's job, so the trainee gets server training as well as a broader picture of the activities that occur in the dining room.

Alter the Training Schedule as Necessary

The training schedule may need to be adjusted based on the ability and experience of the trainee. For example, many foodservice establishments hire employees who are learning-impaired. These people take a longer time to learn the job, but once they have mastered it, many turn out to be reliable, competent workers. In the case of a slow learner, the training period needs to be extended. On the other hand, an employee who has had prior experience may not take as long to train as a novice. Regardless of the length of time spent training, all trainees should show that they have mastered the tasks their job requires at the completion of the training period.

When the current staff is retrained to upgrade their skills, the training schedule is generally shortened. For example, it is not necessary to teach every detail to veteran servers. However, it is necessary to review those aspects of the job that need improving.

Include Self-instructional Training

Self-instructional training can save some of the trainer's time and place some of the burden of learning on the trainee. Manuals and, if affordable, audiovisual programs can be given to the trainee to study privately. You may want to set up a quiet study area in the restaurant in order to keep expensive training materials on your premises. Training materials do not replace the live trainer, but they can reduce the time the trainee needs to spend with the live trainer, which is especially valuable in seasonal or other operations in which a sizable amount of training is done.

A Word on Lesson Plans

A lesson plan is a blueprint the trainer follows in conducting a training session. In individualized instruction the trainer has the job checklist, the training manual, and the training schedule with which to contend. While a lesson plan can be an added value, it is not wise to overburden the trainer with yet another document. The training manual can serve as the book of lesson plans, because the tasks it describes are the lessons the trainer needs to teach. The trainer who desires to do so can write notes in the training manual on how to teach the tasks.

Lesson plans become more necessary in group instruction when the trainer may not wish to be extemporaneous, but would rather plan the instruction in advance. The lesson plan can do more than describe how to perform the task, which is indicated in the training manual. The lesson plan can also tell the trainer the props to use, the questions to ask the trainee, and the method to use to teach and test the trainee. Refer to the lesson plan for teaching how to serve wine at the table given in Figure 7-4. This kind of lesson plan can be used for individualized or group instruction.

Figure 7-4. Trainer's lesson plan.

[This lesson plan may be used for individualized instruction or for addressing a group of trainees. If presenting the lesson to a group, provide enough "dummy" bottles for everyone to practice as you explain and demonstrate the task, or have one person in the group come up and practice along with you. Ask questions of the entire group. At the end, have another member of the group come up and practice the entire task.]

TITLE OF LESSON

How to Serve Wine

MATERIALS NEEDED

4 "dummy" wine bottles (empty and capped)
2 waiter's corkscrews
2 linen napkins
2 side towels
8 wine glasses
wine chiller

HOW I WILL PRESENT THE LESSON

I'll explain the procedure step-by-step, stopping often to demonstrate and to have the trainee practice. At the end, I'll ask review questions and have the trainee practice the entire task until he does it correctly without my help.

STEPS TO TEACH AND QUESTIONS TO ASK

1. Explain where to place reds and chilled wines.
   Why open reds before service and allow them to breathe?

2. Present wine to the host.
   Why present the label to the host?

Figure 7-4. *(continued)*

---

3. Remove the lead (or plastic) cap.
   Where would you place the cap after you've removed it?

4. Remove the cork.
   Why should we be careful not to penetrate the cork completely?

   Why is it important to pull the cork out straight and not angle it?

5. Present the cork to the host.

6. Wipe the lip of the bottle and pour a taste for the host.

7. Serve the guests.
   Who should you serve first? Last?

   Why should you be careful not to shake or jostle the wine?

   Why do we not fill the glasses completely?

   Why do we turn the bottle on the last drop?

REVIEW QUESTIONS TO ASK THE TRAINEE

1. What's the first thing you would do when you bring the wine to the table?

2. How would you remove the lead cap?

3. Explain to me how you would remove the cork.

4. What would you do next?

5. How would you serve the wine?

TEST THE TRAINEE

I'll pretend to be the guest and I'll have the trainee open a bottle of wine and serve it to me.

Monitor Training

You should monitor trainers to be sure they are doing a good job. The ways in which you can monitor the training include (1) observing the trainers while they are teaching, (2) talking to the trainees about how their training is progressing, and (3) evaluating the results—the performance of the trainees who have been trained. Refer to the checklist for evaluating the trainer in Figure 7-5 for the criteria to use in appraising the performance of your trainers.

Figure 7-5. Checklist for evaluating the trainer.

ATTITUDE

How was the trainer's manner? Was he patient, pleasant? Did he put the trainee at ease? Did he encourage questions?

INTRODUCTION

1. Did the trainer clearly state what he was going to show the trainee to do?

2. Did the trainer tell why the task was important?

TEACHING

1. Did the trainer break the task down into steps so the trainee could grasp them?

2. Did the trainer try to explain each step? Was his explanation clear?

3. Did the trainer demonstrate the steps for the trainee?

4. Did the trainer allow the trainee time to practice the steps?

5. Was the trainer skillful at using questions to get the trainee to pay attention and learn more effectively?

TESTING

Did the trainer test the trainee to be sure he could actually perform the entire task himself?

OVERALL

What is your overall evaluation of this trainer? What are his strong points and in what ways might he improve?

Individualized instruction is very valuable for persons who are new to a job. A trainer who is skilled at the proper techniques for teaching someone a job can produce competent and enthusiastic employees for you.

Summary

Individualized instruction by a trainer is an excellent way to learn a new job. The following are guidelines for training a new employee one-on-one: (1) respect the trainee; (2) teach tasks one at a time; (3) explain, demonstrate, and have the trainee practice each task; (4) test the trainee; (5) design a training schedule; (6) include self-instructional training; and (7) monitor the training.

Giving reasons and asking the trainee questions are two important techniques in explaining the task clearly. Demonstrating the task gives the trainee a proper role model to emulate. The trainee should practice the task until able to do it correctly without guidance. The trainee's knowledge and performance should be tested through written quizzes and through performance evaluations. The training schedule is your way of controlling the trainer's and trainee's time. The schedule should include on-the-job and off-the-job training, it should train from simple tasks to complex ones, it may include cross-training, and it should be altered as necessary, depending on the ability and experience of the trainee.

8

Group Instruction

It is sometimes necessary to conduct training for a group. A large number of trainees may be hired at one time, or the current staff may collectively need training or retraining. These are occasions for meetings. Although we said that private instruction is a more effective way to learn, it sometimes is not feasible. There is simply a finite amount of time, and if you have many trainees, group instruction for much of the training will be more practical.

Group instruction can be very enjoyable and beneficial. This chapter will give you some ideas on setting up a training meeting and the kind of meeting to hold to best accomplish your objectives.

The Logistics of Holding Meetings

The following are some things to consider in giving an effective presentation.

Plan the Meeting

You should have a specific purpose in mind in holding the meeting. Develop an agenda or list of points to be covered at the meeting. You may also want to give a copy of the agenda to each person in the audience. A well-planned meeting that moves along, sticks to its agenda, and achieves its purpose is usually enjoyed by the speaker and the audience. The same rules for limiting the subject matter and presenting it in a stepwise fashion that were described in giving individualized instruction also pertain to training groups.

Be an Interesting Speaker

In addition to being well prepared, a speaker must speak loudly and clearly and must exude enthusiasm in order to hold the audience's attention. It is often a challenge to hold attention when a meeting is held in a restaurant, where the lighting and seating are not ideal and where there are often distractions. Being loud, clear and animated is important in holding attention. This usually requires standing, which will feel awkward if you are not used to it. Nevertheless, standing while you speak does become natural with practice.

It is also important to project to the group that the subject is fun and interesting. This is done through your enthusiasm. A certain amount of acting may be involved because, if you are like most of us, you will not necessarily feel enthusiastic all of the time. One thing that helps a speaker maintain enthusiasm is to resolve not to be adversely affected by cynicism in the group. It is common for employees to complain about having to attend meetings, and the speaker should not take this personally. Of course, if there is a serious problem that needs to be addressed, it would be unwise to ignore it. However, a certain amount of complaining and skepticism about meetings is standard, except in the newest and most humble employees. You can influence the negative attitudes of employees by conducting a meeting that is informative, interesting, and enthusiastically presented, rather than by allowing their lack of interest to extinguish your enthusiasm.

Any instructor who can skillfully use humor can be quite entertaining. Humor is a definite plus. However, it needs to be natural and not contrived. The humor can come almost "by itself," naturally, when the speaker feels confident about the presentation. Humor entertains the audience while you educate them, which makes the learning more enjoyable.

Use Training Aids

Handouts or sections of the training manual can help the group better understand the points. If the subject is complex or very detailed, written information is essential in the employees' retaining the points. For example, if you hold a meeting on the menu, and you go through the ingredients in and preparation of each menu item in detail, the meeting might be interesting and informative. However, much of the information will be forgotten if you have not provided a written handout. Do not rely on the employees to take notes and catch every point. Give them a handout to study and, at the next meeting, quiz them to see if they have learned the material. In many cases information, such as knowledge of each menu item, simply has to be memorized, and a quiz will motivate the group to study the information. If you have gone through the effort and expense of having a meeting about an important subject, it is wise to hold the employees accountable for learning the information you presented.

You may also want to use a flip chart or blackboard to write down points for emphasis.

In addition, audiovisual aids may fit into your agenda. Slides and video programs can help dramatize your message and add interest.

Arrange the Setting

The lights should be turned up as much as possible, music should be cut, and seats should be arranged so everyone is close to the speaker. Do not allow people to fall asleep in out-of-the-way booths while you are speaking. Distracting noises from other employees working nearby should be minimized. Sometimes it is a real challenge to create good meeting conditions within a restaurant. Remember the money it costs you to run a meeting, and take a few extra moments to make the conditions suitable for learning.

Have the Managers Attend

If someone other than the manager is giving the presentation, such as someone from the corporate staff, the local restaurant association, or a supplier, the managers should be sure to attend. Your presence projects to the staff that you are interested and take the subject seriously. If you and the other managers are absent from key meetings, the staff will often conclude that you are disinterested. You will also need to know what the staff has been told so you can follow up with them on the job. Invariably there will be some points raised during the meeting that only you can answer. Your absence puts the speaker at a great disadvantage when he or she cannot answer a question and has no manager to turn to for an answer. The staff will also feel neglected if they have questions they need to address to you.

Types of Meetings

The type of meeting you hold should depend on your purpose. The ultimate purpose of any training meeting is, of course, to improve performance.

However, performance can be influenced either directly or indirectly. Meetings can be thought of in terms of whether you intend to influence performance indirectly, by giving information needed to improve job skills, or whether you intend to influence performance directly, by engaging the group in skill-building exercises. If your purpose is to inform the group about matters important to their work, then a presentation in which the instructor is primarily active is appropriate because the instructor has information that needs to be communicated to the group. This type of presentation is basically lecture-style. If your purpose is to directly sharpen the skills of your employees, then the format should be one that allows for practice and skill building, which will primarily be class-active. Or, you can hold a meeting that combines both of these elements, such as a meeting in which an instructor presents a subject and then the class practices applying the information. Knowledge relevant to the job and the application of that knowledge are both important in improving performance, and both types of meetings are needed.

Lecture-Style Meetings

Sometimes the information that needs to be presented is extensive and a lecture-style meeting is the most efficient way to communicate this information to the group. For example, there may be a new wine list, new register equipment, or a new menu that must be explained. The staff needs to listen and absorb the information.

Lectures can be excellent ways of learning. I do not agree with the popular trend to derogate lectures in favor of group discussion-type meetings. For example, if a wine expert lectures the group, in one hour your employees can learn more from the specialist than they could learn by talking to themselves endlessly (assuming they are not wine experts). In a meeting of this nature it would be a useless waste of time to have much class discussion, because the value of the meeting is in hearing the expert speak, not themselves. When presented in an interesting fashion by a good speaker, lectures can be very enjoyable. However, the lecturer should be an expert on the topic he or she is discussing, be it first aid, sanitation, menu, wine, service, or whatever. The lecturer's knowledge of the subject makes the lecture interesting to hear.

The subject also needs to be relevant to the group if the presentation is to be of interest to them. Motivating the audience at the beginning is essential in capturing their interest. Remind the group of the importance to them of the subject that will be addressed. For example, remind bussers of the chance to be promoted to waiter if they do a good job, remind servers of the increase in tips they can get with improved suggestive selling, and remind cooks of how much easier their job is when the orders are cooked properly and there are no returns.

Of course, even in purely lecture-type presentations, you should allow questions from the group. Depending on the group, these questions may come during the presentation or you may ask the group to hold their questions until the end. After giving countless lectures to groups of all sizes, I have observed the following regarding the group's asking questions.

Having the group hold its questions until the end has several advantages. It is more efficient, enabling you to cover your points in the shortest amount of time. It makes your presentation more integrated and more compelling when your train of thought is not interrupted by questions. Very often questions will be asked that anticipate points you plan to cover, and answering them out of the sequence in which you intend to make the points dilutes the presentation.

Having the group hold questions until the end also helps in controlling the group. Some groups are disorderly, often due to their immaturity or lack of experience attending meetings. These groups will entirely dominate the meeting if you allow them to ask questions whenever they feel like it. As a result, you will lose control of the group and not have time to get your points across. You will also find yourself shouting over their voices. When a group is disorderly, I will automatically go into a lecture-style presentation even if I had not originally planned that approach.

Sometimes it is advantageous to have the group ask questions or make comments during the presentation. When the group is ominously quiet, especially if it is a small group, I often feel I cannot go on until they have made some utterance. I will sometimes stop and ask each member to say something. For example, if I am discussing customer service with a group of bussers who seem utterly disinterested, I will stop and call on each of them to give me one good tip on giving customer service, or I will ask each one to relate an experience in which the guest directly tipped him. This "breaks the ice." It does no good, I have found, to throw general questions out to a group that is ominously quiet, because no one will raise a hand to answer them. It is better to say, "I'm going to go around the room and ask each of you to tell me . . . " or to simply call on people at random to answer your questions.

Having the group ask questions during your presentation also has the advantage of clarifying any points they do not understand. The problem is that they will also ask questions on points you plan to make at a later time or on tangential issues you do not want to address at that moment. You might say that you will answer questions of clarification during the presentation and ask them to hold other questions that do not directly relate to the point you are making until the end. This is not cruel, believe me. It is better for them and for you.

Include as much demonstration as possible in your lecture. If you are discussing some new menu items, cook them, if possible, and have the staff taste them. You may want to conduct part of the class in the dining room and then go into the kitchen for the demonstrations.

A lecture-style meeting does not imply that the class is silent; it means that the instructor is doing most of the talking because he or she is imparting needed information to the group.

Application-Style Meetings

Sometimes the information you have to communicate is very simple and what is really needed by the group is practice. For example, consider a restaurant in which the bussers are a young, "green" staff. They do not clear the table properly. Let us assume it takes them four trips to the table to clear and reset. What is needed at a bussers' meeting to correct this problem is practice. It would only take five or ten minutes for an instructor to explain and demonstrate how the table should be cleared. The rest of the meeting time should be devoted to practice.

You could arrange to have a group of tables nearby that need clearing and resetting. Have each busser clear one while the others watch. Time the busser and have the person give a self-critique of his or her speed and accuracy. The class should also critique each busser's performance. This type of meeting is devoted to directly building skills. Little talking by a lecturer is necessary. What is needed is proficiency in a task.

The class can be called upon to help each other improve. In role-playing and other skill-building exercises, members of the class can help in evaluating one another's performance. However, class critiques of an individual's performance need to be presented in a very constructive way. You may want the class to indicate the positive aspects of the performance first, then give suggestions for improvement. Criticism should pertain to a worker's actions and not be a slur against the person's intelligence or character. You may also want to state and repeat as necessary to the group that the purpose of the skill-building exercises is to help everyone improve and that they should not take criticisms personally (that is, defensively). You may also invite them to make suggestions to you for improving the operation with your assurance that, if the suggestions are presented constructively, you will not take them personally, but consider them seriously. (Refer to the section on giving constructive criticism in Chapter 11 and apply these guidelines to your group meetings.)

The Combined Approach

Very often the same meeting will combine knowledge and application. (Or this will be done in two meetings, where the first is devoted to giving information to the group and the second is devoted to their applying the information.)

For example, consider a meeting with servers in which the techniques of suggestive selling are first presented, then the group practices the techniques in role-play exercises.

A Word on the Figures

Figure 8-1 is a handy form for keeping track of the training needs of an entire department.

Figure 8-2 is the agenda of a very enjoyable and effective two-hour meeting for hostesses. This meeting was application-style. The purpose was to remind the hostesses of the importance of hospitality and to encourage them to practice hospitality in the daily situations they faced. (Hospitality is one of those subjects that does not require a long dissertation to be understood; it requires instances and examples of how to show hospitality to guests.)

The meeting began with a film and some pointers on service, presented by the manager, but most of the meeting was devoted to the group's practicing hospitality. There were three exercises: (1) role-plays of common situations which were not always handled to the manager's satisfaction; (2) an exercise in which each member of the group was asked to offer one good idea on making the guests feel welcomed; and (3) an exercise in which a series of difficult situations were discussed with the group and they were asked how they would handle each one.

Figure 8-3 gives the role-play exercises. In each situation, one person played the hostess and one (or two) persons played the guests. The players were only shown their own respective parts. The other class members were shown both parts, so they knew the context of both the hostess and the guests. The players enacted the role-play for the group, then it was discussed under the manager's guidance. This was done for each of the five role-plays.

Figure 8-4 describes the last exercise of the meeting, the problem situations that were discussed by the hostesses.

This meeting offers three different types of application exercises on the subject of hospitality. I organized this meeting for H. Brinker's, a popular restaurant in Denver that kindly gave me permission to reproduce the training materials here.

Figure 8-1. Training plan and record. (Courtesy of Inhilco, Inc.)

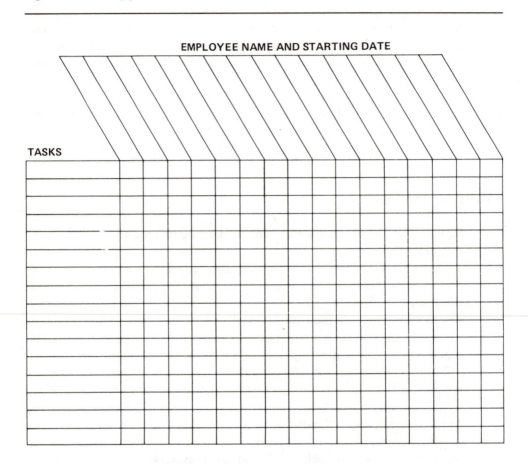

EMPLOYEE NAME AND STARTING DATE

TASKS

To use this plan:

1. List tasks along the left side.

2. List employees' names and starting dates at the top.

3. Cross through squares where the employees do not need to carry out the tasks. ·

4. Check squares where employees are already up to standards.

5. Initial and date squares when training is given.

BLANK SQUARES INDICATE YOUR TRAINING NEEDS

Figure 8-2. Hostess meeting: agenda. (Courtesy of H. Brinker's.)

AGENDA

1. FILM ON GUEST RELATIONS

2. WHAT YOUR JOB'S ALL ABOUT

3. ROLE PLAYS—WHAT WOULD YOU DO IF . . .

4. GOOD IDEAS TO MAKE GUESTS FEEL WELCOME

5. HANDLING DIFFICULT SITUATIONS—WHAT WOULD YOU DO
    BESIDES SCREAM??????????

Figure 8-3. Hostess meeting: role-plays. (Courtesy of H. Brinker's.)

ROLE-PLAY #1
Hostess

It's been a really hectic Sunday afternoon and you're feeling frazzled. You've got parties everywhere waiting to be seated. You're trying to find a party so you can take them to a table. Just then, two guests come out of the dining room and approach you, looking annoyed.

Guests

This is the first time you've been to H. Brinker's. It's a Sunday and you've come for brunch. You enjoyed the brunch very much; however, the restaurant was quite crowded and there were some delays in service.

You've got an appointment to meet friends downtown and it's getting late. You're annoyed that your server dropped the check on the table and has disappeared for 10 minutes. You get up and take the bill to the hostess station. You're annoyed and you want the hostess to help you.

If the hostess refuses to help, you're going to make a fuss. By now, you're late for your appointment.

ROLE-PLAY #2
Hostess

It's been a busy evening. It's late and you're tired. Two guests are walking out the door. As they go, you bid them goodnight.

Figure 8-3. *(continued)*

Guests

You just spent $60 for dinner and wine. You've been out of work and money's been tight. You're celebrating your first wedding anniversary, and it's the first time you've dined out in months. You thought the food was good, but the service was bad. You don't want to make a big deal about it and ruin the evening so you haven't said anything, but it bugs you. On an impulse, you make a remark about the bad service to the hostess on the way out the door.

You don't know why you made the remark to the hostess. You don't want to see a manager or make a fuss about it, yet you feel you should have been treated better. You don't know what you'd like the hostess to do.

ROLE-PLAY #3
Hostess

You're walking with a party through the dining room. You're taking them to a table that's near the kitchen. All of a sudden the party stops walking with you. They're looking at an empty table by the window. The table has not been bussed yet.

Guests

The hostess is taking you through the dining room to your table. It is apparent that you're going to be seated at a table near the kitchen. All of a sudden, you spot a party leaving. Their table is near the window, and you'd much prefer to sit there. You're going to ask the hostess about sitting at the window table. If the hostess refuses, you're going to get angry. After all, you're a steady customer and you've waited 45 minutes for a table. You want a nice one.

ROLE-PLAY #4
Hostess

It's 11:00 A.M. on a Thursday. You've already gotten a number of reservations for lunch, and you expect to be busy. The phone rings and you answer it.

Caller

It's 11:00 A.M. on a Thursday and you're in your office. You've just been asked by your boss to take some out-of-town clients to lunch. There will be eight people going to lunch. Your boss says he's sorry for forgetting to tell you about the lunch earlier, but, he adds, it's an important account and the lunch had better be good.

You call H. Brinker's to make a reservation for eight at 12:00. You're in a bind. You're a steady customer at Brinker's and you expect them to accommodate you.

ROLE-PLAY #5
Hostess

The phone rings. This is the third time in the last half hour that this person has called asking you to page someone in the restaurant. You've already explained that you can't page someone while the piano player is performing. The piano player is still performing when you receive the third call.

Caller

You're babysitting for your sister's kids while you're studying for final exams. You didn't want to babysit, but you're doing your sister a favor, so she and her husband can go out to dinner to celebrate her birthday. You're trying to study, but the baby keeps crying. Your sister said the baby has a favorite toy that usually makes him stop crying. You need to find out where the toy is.

You try to reach your sister, who's having dinner at H. Brinker's. You've called twice and were told the piano player was performing and they couldn't page your sister until he was through. Your exam is tomorrow, you're not getting any work done, and you're frantic. You call the restaurant a third time. This time you're determined to speak to your sister.

Figure 8-4. Hostess meeting: handling difficult situations. (Courtesy of H. Brinker's.)

How would you handle each of the following situations?

1. A party of four walks in and insists that it made a reservation, although there is no record of it. At the time there is a 30-minute wait. What would you say to the guests?

_____
_____
_____

2. A server screams at you for seating a party in her station just as she was trying to close her station and leave for the night. What would you do? What exactly would you say to the server?

_____
_____
_____

3. As they are leaving, some guests complain to you that they really didn't enjoy themselves. The food wasn't very good and the service was slow. What would you say to the guests?

_____
_____
_____

Figure 8-4. *(continued)*

---

4. You tell an arriving party that there will be a one-hour wait. One of the guests belligerently says, "What do you mean a one-hour wait, on a Thursday night?" What would you reply?

_____

_____

5. There is a 45-minute wait. A couple in the lounge keeps pressuring you to seat them. They still have many couples ahead of them. What would you do? What would you say to them?

_____

_____

6. A person in the lounge is looking very faint. He tells you he's a diabetic and is about to go into insulin shock. What would you do?

_____

_____

In conclusion, group instruction is a practical way of training a number of employees. For it to work, your meetings must be properly planned and conducted.

SUMMARY

Sometimes there are a large number of trainees and group instruction is the most practical means of training them. The following are some of the logistics to consider in holding effective meetings: (1) Plan the meeting; (2) be an interesting speaker; (3) use written, visual, and audiovisual training aids; (4) arrange the seating, lighting, and the rest of the setting so it is conducive to learning; and (5) have the managers attend the meetings.

The ultimate purpose of all training meetings is to improve performance. This can be accomplished either indirectly, when information is given to employees so that they can do a better job, or directly, when the meeting concentrates specifically on building the skills of the employees. Two popular types of meetings are lecture-style and application-style. Lecture-style imparts job-related information to the group and indirectly improves their skills. Application-style uses exercises to directly build skills during the meeting. Both kinds of meetings are important, because knowledge relevant to the job and application of that knowledge are both important in job performance. A combination of both approaches in the same meeting is also possible.

9

Using Audiovisuals

Audiovisual programs are those that are available on slide-tape, filmstrip, videotape, or motion picture film. True to their name, they have both a visual and an audio component. They are widely used in training foodservice employees. Virtually all the large chains have custom-designed audiovisual programs for job skills training. Programs for cooks, dishwashers, servers, and all other members of the staff showing how to perform the tasks of their jobs are common in most of the large chains. Many independents use generic video training programs that are commercially available. The reasons for the popularity of audiovisual programs are:

1. They make learning easier for the trainee.

Audiovisual programs are fun to watch. Whenever you can add interest to the training program, the learning becomes less of a chore and more enjoyable. Audiovisuals make the learning interesting and entertaining. They also make the learning more pleasant by reducing the reading time for the trainee. You do not have to go into as much detail in your training manuals when you have audiovisual programs that explain and demonstrate tasks. The reduced reading time is welcomed by many trainees.

2. They make teaching easier for the trainer.

While they do not replace the live trainer, audiovisual programs can greatly aid the training and make part of it self-instructional. There is no replacement for a live trainer who can answer questions, clarify confusions, and supervise the trainee's performance. However, audiovisual programs make it possible to save a great deal of the trainer's time and to insure consistency and completeness in training by introducing the basic skills through the programs.

3. They make controlling the training easier for the owner or manager.

Audiovisual programs provide a correct and consistent role model. An audiovisual program can accomplish what a training manual cannot—it can show a role model correctly performing the skills under study for the trainee to emulate. You can be assured that the audiovisual role model will consistently perform the same way, whereas live trainers may or may not provide the proper role model.

The best kind of audio-visual programs are those that are custom-designed for your operation. However, these can be expensive to produce and usually become cost-effective only when there are multiple units of the same concept with all units sharing in the cost, thus driving down the expense for any one operation.

Aside from their cost, another disadvantage of custom-designed programs is their becoming outdated. For example, a company completes an orientation program that describes one of its major divisions, and a month later the division is sold. Or a new menu is instituted and the items mentioned in the audiovisual program no longer exist. Either revisions can be made or the subject matter can be chosen carefully to try to avoid mentioning people or topics that are likely to change.

A less expensive route is to choose commercially available programs. These programs are primarily in the video format, and they are becoming more and more popular. We will probably see a wider variety of commercially available videotapes for training foodservice employees in the years to come. A drawback to generic programs is that they may not fully apply to your particular operation.

Things to Consider in Making Your Own Programs

If you decide to make your own audiovisual programs, you should consider hiring a production company to assist you. It can become far more complicated than you think to produce a good-quality program. The following are some of the considerations involved in producing your own audiovisual programs.

Determine the Budget

How much money can you spend on audiovisual programs? Assume a typical audiovisual program will have a life span of five years. How many employees will you train using that program over a five-year period? Figure out the cost per employee of using the program for a five-year period, based on the projected number of employees who will see the program and the estimated cost of producing the program (based on bids from production companies). Can you afford the program? If there are other restaurants in your company, the costs can be disseminated among all of those operations that will use the program.

If you do not have the budget to produce your own audiovisual programs, be assured that you can do a completely adequate job of training with your written materials and live trainers. The training may take longer, require more of the trainer's time, and be more difficult to monitor, but the quality of the instruction can be good without the use of audiovisuals. Remember that audiovisuals are an excellent way of communicating your job standards, but they are not the only way.

Choose the Topics for the Programs

Do you want a tape on service to show to all servers? Do you want a program on sanitation? An orientation program? A program on hospitality? Many topics lend themselves to audiovisual presentation. Stay away from naming all the company executives, the menu items, and the prices because these things can change. It is better to treat information that changes frequently in your manuals, where changes will be easier and less expensive to make (especially if the manuals are in a loose-leaf format).

If you can only produce one or a few programs, choose topics that will have wide-scale applicability. For example, an orientation program will be shown to all new employees, as will a program on guest awareness, which concentrates on how each employee contributes to the guest's enjoyment. Another popular topic is service, because the servers in many restaurants comprise the bulk of the staff and there is high turnover in that position. Another popular topic is sanitation. A sanitation program can also be shown to all employees. Some companies will have the budget to systematically put all job skills on an audiovisual format and train for each position using a combination of audiovisual programs, manuals, and the live trainer giving one-on-one instruction.

It is important to limit the subject matter so you do not include too much in one program. An audiovisual program should generally run 10 to 20 minutes. How much can be covered in that time span? You can get a fairly good description of a particular position on a program of 10 to 20 minutes if the job is not too complex. One company chose to produce one program that explained the entire server's job; however, it found that writing guest checks was too complex to be included. A separate program of about ten minutes was produced on writing and reading the guest check. The guest check program was used to train cooks as well as servers.

Decide on the Equipment to Use

Videotape presentations require a videotape player and monitor to view. There is equipment available that has the monitor and player in one compact unit. Slides can be shown on either a slide-tape projector, a filmstrip projector, or a videocassette player.

Slide-tape projectors are available that allow individuals and small groups to view the slides on a small built-in screen or to project the images on a larger screen for large groups. These slide projectors also have a built-in audiocassette recorder for the accompanying audiotape.

Slides may be transferred to a filmstrip format that shows all of the slides on a continuous strip of film. This strip of film can be put into a cartridge with the sound included and shown on a filmstrip projector. These projectors are lightweight and also have the option of showing the image on the small built-in screen for individual trainees or on a larger screen for group presentations.

Slides may also be transferred to video and shown on a videocassette player. If you are often training large groups with slide presentations, slide-tape and filmstrip projectors are better than video. A videotape loses resolution when shown on a big screen and furthermore, large video screens are expensive to rent or buy. Motion picture film is excellent when projected on a large screen for groups; however, film is more expensive than video to produce and to duplicate for distribution.

A filmstrip projector has an advantage over a slide-tape projector or videocassette player because it has no use outside of the restaurant and is far less likely to be stolen. The filmstrip projector is also the least expensive of the three formats. Keeping the slides in a slide tray instead of transferring them to a filmstrip or videocassette has the advantage of allowing you to update slides. For example, if you have a series of slides depicting coffee service, and you have changed the coffee pots you use, you can replace those slides with up-to-date ones showing the current equipment when the slides are sitting in a tray. Slides in a tray, however, are more likely to be dropped, lost, stolen, soiled, or otherwise damaged.

Consider transferring slide shows to video if you are planning to supplement your slide shows with commercially available video training tapes or with video programs you plan to produce in-house. This way you will only need the one set of equipment, the videocassette recorder and monitor, for all your programs. Contact your local production studios and equipment dealers for prices on equipment and on the cost of transferring slide shows to different formats.

There are advantages and disadvantages to using any piece of equipment. The best choice depends on your budget and needs.

Decide on the Format

Should it be a slide-tape show or a video production? The answer to this question depends on the subject matter and the budget. A slide show is usually less expensive to produce than a video presentation, because photography and slide editing are less complicated and costly than videography.

Regarding the subject, virtually all restaurant skills training could be done with either still frames (slides) or motion (video).

Video generally has advantages over slides. The motion makes the show more realistic. Whenever the training depicts dialogue with the customer, video is markedly superior. While slides are good at showing motor skills, they really fall short when it comes to dialogue. On slides, dialogue seems unrealistic and contrived. Video is far better at showing hostesses greeting guests, servers taking orders and using suggestive selling techniques, and staff members handling customer complaints. When slides are used, a voice-over narrator, someone offscreen who describes what is going on in the pictures, should be used and on-camera dialogue should be avoided as much as possible. (Of course, it will be impossible to avoid dialogue when teaching communication skills, such as handling a guest complaint. However, in the teaching of motor skills, like making a sandwich or operating the dish machine, dialogue can be avoided when using slides.)

For showing motor skills, video has the advantage of being able to show the smooth flow of motions from beginning to end. Slides, however, can freeze the motion and isolate a particular action on which the trainee can focus. For example, if you are showing how to slice an onion, slides can stop the motion just as the knife is slicing the onion while a narrator describes the technique. The trainee gets a chance to study the pose. (Of course, in a video program, still pictures or slow motion can always be included which would freeze the motion and give the viewer an opportunity to study the pose.)

If you do not have the budget to put all your training on video and would like to use a combination of slide and video in the same or different programs, reserve video for customer service skills and use slides for those tasks that basically involve motor skills. You can transfer your slide shows to videotape so that you can use a videocassette player for both the slide and motion programs. Having the slides on videotape also gives you the opportunity to edit live motion into your show.

Stages of Production

If you decide to produce your own audiovisual programs, you will most likely be working with a production company. It will be easier for you and the company if you assign either yourself or another manager to be the liason with the production company. The liason should have the authority to approve the script, arrange for the shooting, and make those decisions necessary to get the program produced, such as the choice of narrator, talent, graphics, and so forth.

The following are the stages that you and the production company will have to go through. These stages are essentially the same for video and slide shows.

Stage One: Preproduction

Preproduction is the planning stage. The more carefully the planning is done, the better will be the end product. Once the budget, subject matter, and medium are decided upon, you can begin to plan the particular show. The planning involves writing the script, choosing the shooting locations, securing the props and product, selecting the talent, and setting the shooting schedule.

Writing the Script

First, the scriptwriter should prepare an outline of the points to be covered in the show. Once the outline is approved, the narrative script should be written. This script indicates what is said by the narrator and by any on-camera speakers. Once the narrative script is approved, a shooting script or story-board is produced, which describes or shows the way the script is to be shot. The shooting script *describes* the shots while a storyboard *illustrates* the shots. Either a shooting script or a storyboard may be used in producing the show. Both the narrative and shooting script (or storyboard) should be finalized and approved before production.

Choosing the Shooting Locations and Securing the Props and Product

If more than one restaurant will be using the show, the restaurant that is best for the shooting should be selected. An attractive and clean setting, room to shoot, and hours of operation should be considered when choosing among restaurants. If one restaurant is closed for lunch, for example, consider doing the shooting there in the early mornings and afternoon. The props include uniforms, utensils, and equipment necessary for the shoot. Uniforms should be new and all props and locations should be very clean so that a professional image is projected in the show. The operator should also be prepared for the expense of using product as needed in the show.

Selecting the Talent

Employees do a fine job in parts that do not involve on-camera speaking. For example, in slide and video shows in which employees' actions are described by a narrator, you can feel confident in using your own employees for the production. Consider using professional talent for the narration and for any parts that require a fair amount of speaking. Employees are usually uncomfortable speaking on camera and come across as being ill at ease, which they are. In many shows extras are needed to act as customers. Again, if speaking is not required, these people can be employees or friends. (All talent should sign a "release," giving you permission to use them in your in-house training programs.)

Setting the Shooting Schedule

The production will be very disruptive to the operation, with lights, cameras, technicians, and actors scurrying around. For this reason, the shooting is typically done when the restaurant is closed. In some cases this can require shooting from 11 P.M. to 7 A.M. The players, location, props, and product will all have to be secured for the times of shooting.

Stage Two: Production

Once the plans are completed and all the preproduction arrangements have been made, you are ready to shoot. The camera crew will shoot in sections, so if the same setting appears several times in your show, all shots of it will probably be taken at one time, even though they will appear in different segments of your show. Shooting takes time. Lights and equipment have to be set up for each shot. Several pictures or "takes" have to be done of each sequence. A good production crew may take a long time to get things just right, but the results will be worth the extra time.

Stage Three: Postproduction

After the shooting is completed, the slides or videotape sequences have to be edited. The right slides or scenes have to be selected and arranged in the proper order for the show. Titles, company logo, and other graphics work is also done during postproduction. The sound track has to be produced, consisting of the narration, music, and sound effects. At the end of this whole process, you have your finished show!

Figure 9-1 is the beginning of the script of a commercially available sales training video for servers, entitled "The Professional Server: How to Increase Sales and Tips." The right-hand column is the audio cue, or dialogue. The

Figure 9-1. Script from "The Professional Server: How to Increase Sales and Tips." (Sponsor: *Restaurant Business* Magazine. Writer: Gen LaGreca.)

THE PROFESSIONAL SERVER: HOW TO INCREASE SALES AND TIPS

INTRODUCTION

When the show opens, we are looking at the dining room of the restaurant, crowded with people. We see the restaurant from the point of view of Julie Peters, who is a former waitress there and the star of the show. She is going to tell her story as a flashback. (We don't see Julie at the present time until the end of the show.) The camera should show the activity of the restaurant as the show is introduced. We should see the action and hear the noises of a busy restaurant.

JULIE'S VOICEOVER   This place holds many memories for me. It was here that I spent my school years waitressing. And it was here that I learned a lot about waitressing, about making money, . . . and about myself.

SCENE 1

The action switches to outside the manager's office. The manager, Bob Reed, comes out of his office and looks around for Julie. Bob is an intelligent-looking man in his thirties or forties, well-dressed in a business suit.

JULIE'S VOICEOVER   It all started the day my manager called me into his office.

BOB
Sees Julie and motions to her. Other servers should be walking about, also. We still do not see Julie.

Julie, have a few minutes? . . . Come in, please.

JULIE'S VOICEOVER
The camera walks with Julie into Bob's office. Bob follows and they both sit down.

I wondered what was on Bob's mind. I had only worked there a few weeks, but I was a good waitress. Surely, it couldn't be my performance.

BOB

Julie, I'd like to talk to you about your performance.

JULIE
We see Julie for the first time. She looks like a timid librarian—hair unstyled and pulled back in a bun, blouse wrinkled, thick black-rimmed glasses, no make-up and slouching. (Although she shouldn't look so bad that it's unbelievable that she would have been hired. I'd like to get a laugh here, because when we see her, it's obvious she's not doing as well as she thinks.)

What do you mean?

BOB
He's frank, but kind. He takes out some sheets of paper and looks something up.

I'm concerned about your sales. Remember when you were hired, and I told you that you'd be expected to maintain a certain level of sales?

JULIE
A little scared and uncomfortable.

Yes.

BOB

Well, my records show that your sales are a dollar per customer lower than the average server's.

He hands the sheets to Julie and points out the lines for her to look at. Julie looks them over, then gives them back.

Bob points to figures on the sheets.

And by having low sales, your tips suffer, too.

JULIE
Defensively.

But, I try to sell.

BOB
Skeptical

Do you?

JULIE

Well, sometimes.

Figure 9-1. *(continued)*

BOB
Raises his eyebrows, skeptically.

JULIE   Actually, I don't feel right about push-
                                         ing food and drinks on people.

BOB   Don't you think you can suggest things
                                         tastefully without making your guests
                                         feel pressured to buy?

JULIE
Shrugs her shoulders.

BOB   I'm going to ask you to train with Steve
Bob waits for a response, but Julie   Burton.
gives none. Julie just sinks in her chair
and looks down.

JULIE   Oh no! Not Steve!
Lifts her head and is agitated.

BOB   Why not?

JULIE   He's so . . . stuck up. He won't want to
                                         teach me. I'll never learn from Steve.

BOB   Steve's sales are two dollars per cus-
Looks at the sales sheets.   tomer higher than yours.

Reassuring   And you're wrong about him. He loves
                                         to teach new servers. He's patient and
                                         understanding . . . you'll see.

Camera fades out on Julie's face
dreading what's to come.

SCENE 2

The camera comes in on Steve's face, sitting in the same chair as Julie was in Bob's
office. It's shortly after Bob's conversation with Julie on the same day. Steve and Bob
are now talking in Bob's office.

STEVE   You've got to be kidding! Teach her?
With a look of disbelief. (I'd like to get a
laugh here, just after Bob explains how
kind and understanding Steve is.)

BOB	I think she's good material. She just needs training, and . . .
gropes for words	some confidence in herself.
STEVE	
Looks around, looks up at the ceiling, and says to himself.	(What she needs is another line of work.)
	Allright, I'll try, but don't expect miracles.
BOB	I don't. That's all I'm asking.
STEVE	
Shrugs.	

---

left-hand column is the video cue, describing the shots to be taken. After writing this script, the producer arranged the shots in the order in which it would be easiest to take them, rather than in the order in which they appeared in the show.

This particular video training tape is available through *Restaurant Business* magazine. It is supplemented with a written training guide that includes a summary of the points covered, discussion questions, and a quiz for the servers.

It is a good idea to supplement your audiovisual programs with written materials, or manuals, which the employees read. You probably will not be able to say everything about the job in the audiovisual program, so written materials will still be needed. Some companies will reproduce the scripts of the audiovisual programs in the training manuals, so the employees can review key points and study the program in great detail.

Audiovisual programs are highly recommended for use in training whenever there is a budget for them.

Summary

Audiovisual programs are those that are available on sound-slide, filmstrip, videotape, or motion picture film. They are very popular for training food-service employees because (1) they make learning easier for the trainee, (2) they make teaching easier for the trainer, and (3) they make controlling the training easier for the owner or manager. Companies may chose to custom design their own audiovisual programs or buy commercially available ones. If you decide to make your own programs, the following considerations must be addressed: (1) Determine the budget, (2) choose the topics for the programs, (3) decide on the equipment, and (4) decide on the format. If you decide to produce your own programs, you will more than likely need to hire a production company to help you. There are three basic stages involved in creating your program: preproduction planning, production, and postproduction.

Audiovisual programs, especially custom-designed ones, are highly recommended for training whenever there is a budget for them.

PART SIX

MAINTAINING PERFORMANCE STANDARDS

10

Monitoring Performance

Once the training period is completed, there is a need to continually train and motivate employees in order to maintain performance standards through time. If you fail to closely supervise employees, their performance will slacken off.

For example, consider the case of a coffee shop that trained its servers but failed to maintain performance standards after the training was completed. The servers began working at 6:30 A.M. The problem was their appearance. Most did not take the time to groom at that hour. The men would appear for work unshaven, women with hair uncombed and no makeup applied. Their well-dressed customers, the stockbrokers, lawyers, and investment bankers from the financial district in which the restaurant was located, made the poor appearance of the servers seem even more shabby.

A training program was instituted in which a cosmetician and grooming specialist taught the servers easy techniques for looking presentable at such an early hour. For example, the women were taught ways to apply makeup and style their hair which required little time. Posture and poise were also covered in the training. The training classes were fun and the staff enjoyed them.

The result was an immediate and dramatic improvement in the appearance of the staff. The customers noticed and remarked on how well-groomed the staff looked. However, the improvement was not a lasting one. Slowly, day by day, the staff reverted to their old habits of grooming and after several weeks there were no signs that the training had even taken place. The owner was disappointed and frustrated because he had invested time and money in training with no lasting results to show for it.

Why did this slackening off in appearance occur? There is a great temptation to revert back to old habits. The training period usually is not long enough to form strong new habits. Let's face it, there was a reason why the old habits were formed in the first place: It is easier to compromise in grooming so one can sleep a little later in the morning. Even new employees who have not yet acquired bad habits would be similarly tempted.

How could the slackening off in appearance have been avoided? Here is where the manager plays a crucial role. The reason the employees reverted back to their poor grooming habits was that the manager allowed this to happen. He gave the employees no response, regardless of how well or poorly they were groomed. The manager basically ignored the issue and gave no feedback to employees whether they made the effort to groom correctly or slept late and cut corners. They were neither criticized when their appearance fell short of standards nor praised when their appearance met the standards. How could they take the training seriously if the manager did not take it seriously?

By contrast, another restaurant in the same neighborhood had a reputation for having the most attractive and well-groomed servers in the area. It was no mystery how this was accomplished. The manager lined the servers up before every shift and carefully checked their appearance. Men who were unshaven were sent to the bathroom to shave. Servers whose nails needed scrubbing were sent to the sink with a scrub brush. In this case the standards were enforced and the results were excellent.

Your job is not over when the training period is completed. Ongoing efforts are needed to maintain performance standards. Some important ways in which you can continue to communicate performance standards and motivate employees are as follows:

1. Develop procedures to monitor employee performance and to communicate to employees how they are doing.

2. Develop good human relations skills in dealing with employees.

3. Be a good role model for employees.

These points are the subject of the next three chapters. In this chapter we will discuss the first point: monitoring employee performance.

When you are regularly checking performance and enforcing standards, the employees feel a strong management presence that can profoundly affect their performance. The employees feel you are serious about the standards you set when you make the effort to monitor them. For example, if you tell the kitchen staff to watch food costs, it makes a difference whether you only mention it once every six months at a staff meeting or whether you monitor food costs regularly and direct the staff on how to reduce food costs. The latter approach is the motivating one, the one that will lead to reduced food costs. Since you have the power to retain or fire your employees, your standards are a key factor in motivating your staff. Employees are motivated by what the manager considers important, which they judge by what the manager continually emphasizes and checks.

There are many ways to monitor employee performance. It may be done informally, by observing employees at work, and formally, by establishing procedures for measuring specific aspects of employee performance.

Informal Ways of Monitoring Performance

There is great value in walking around the restaurant, tasting the food, watching the cooking, talking to the guests, observing the service, and so forth. One manager would regularly spend long periods of time in the kitchen, watching the food being prepared and picked up. During the times she was there, the kitchen was a silent, serious place. There were no problems with the orders and no conflicts between cooks and servers. Just as a policeofficer on the street is a deterrent to crime, the alert manager, who watches everything that goes on, exerts a powerful influence on employees' performance.

Some managers feel they have to roll up their sleeves and do dishes, bus tables, and handle other chores as needed. Of course, it is very valuable to spend time performing each job in the restaurant, so you really understand the job and can assist in an emergency. However, as a routine practice, if you are locked into a particular job that an hourly employee could perform, there is a danger of losing sight of the overall context and being unable to perform your function as the overseer. If you have a small department, you can do more hands-on work and still keep track of the overall picture. The larger your domain, the more detrimental it becomes for you to be locked into doing an employee's job.

In order to be effective at monitoring performance informally, your walking around must not be aimless; it must be very purposeful. You must know how to perform each job in the restaurant, so you will know what to look for and be able to evaluate employees fairly as you watch them performing their jobs. You will also need to communicate your reactions to employees in ways that lead to improved performance and not to their resentment and defensiveness. (We will discuss the skills of praising, criticizing, and disciplining employees in a later chapter.)

Make a conscious effort to train yourself to notice as much as possible when you walk through the restaurant. The more alert and perceptive you become, the more adept you will be at monitoring performance informally.

Formal Ways of Monitoring Performance

Formal ways of monitoring performance involve focusing on a particular aspect of job performance and developing specific procedures for monitoring it. A formal system of monitoring performance involves doing more than simply walking around and randomly observing employees. It means that you have a specific factor you want to monitor and a specific means of doing so. One cannot monitor everything, so you must select those aspects of the employees' performance that are problem areas or that are crucial to the success of your operation and monitor them. For example, sales, service, attendance, punctuality, quality of food, waste, breakage, food cost, and cleanliness are some crucial parameters that you may want to monitor carefully.

An example of a formal system for monitoring appearance was already discussed earlier in this chapter. The restaurant that had a reputation for having attractive, well-groomed servers had a formal system for monitoring appearance which had the following features: (1) The manager set specific appearance standards, so the servers knew what to wear and how they were supposed to look. For example, the men had to be clean shaven and everyone had to wear a white shirt that was clean and ironed. (2) The manager devised a method for observing the servers' appearance; that is, he summoned them all to a premeal meeting a few minutes prior to the start of service each day. (3) He gave the servers "feedback" or knowledge of results. If their appearance was acceptable, they were allowed to work, and if it fell short of standards, they were not allowed on the floor until they looked satisfactory. Sometimes this meant shaving, or pulling one's hair back, or cleaning one's apron.

A formal system for monitoring performance involves these three elements:

1. Set goals or standards.

The proper performance needs to be clearly defined, so employees know what is expected of them. Goals or standards should be specific. For example, if a restaurant's average sales per guest are $13, a goal might be to raise the sales to $14. Specifying the dollar amount would make a better goal than merely telling the servers to do their best. The exact dollar amount targets action to a clearly defined result. The goal should be challenging, so it takes effort to achieve. The goal should also be realistic, so employees do not get discouraged by their failure to achieve it.

The purpose of training is to communicate the job standards or goals to the employee and be sure he can perform. Employees need to be trained to meet the standards set. For example, if a manager wants to increase the average check through suggestive selling, the servers should be knowledgeable of the menu, the wine list and suggestive selling techniques. If this kind of training was not done at the time of hire, or if employees need a refresher course, the training should be done as soon as possible so employees will have the knowledge and skills to meet the goals.

2. Measure performance.

A system needs to be developed to measure the employee's performance to see how it compares to the standards or goals. In our example, the server's sales would be measured. The measurement should be fair. In the case of sales, it would not be fair to measure a server's total sales, since this figure will vary by the number of customers served. Sales per customer would be a more equitable measure. (More will be said later in this chapter on measuring server sales.)

3. Give feedback.

Giving feedback means informing employees of how they are doing. Employees need to know whether their performance meets, exceeds, or falls short of the standards set. Employees whose performance falls short need to take corrective action. Those who meet the standards should be told how well they are doing so they can continue the same actions. Those who exceed the standards should be recognized and appreciated for their achievements. It is your responsibility to inform employees of how their performance compares to the goals.

Feedback should be given regularly. Do not wait six months to inform an employee that his or her sales are poor, for example. Little feedback given seldom can hardly have a motivating effect on the employee's daily performance.

In giving feedback, it is desirable to emphasize the positive whenever possible. In the case of sales, an outstanding performance may be honored with an award. The strategy here is to link the employee's self-interest to doing a good job for you. Rewards given for exceptional performance show that you recognize and appreciate the employee's extra efforts and they give something of value, such as a complimentary dinner, a bottle of wine, or an even larger prize.

The following are examples of formal systems for monitoring performance that have been established for restaurant employees. They all involve using the same method: (1) setting standards or goals, and communicating those standards to employees; (2) developing a system for measuring performance; and (3) giving feedback to employees on a regular basis regarding how they are doing. It is important to experiment with different schemes to find the ones that work best in a particular operation.

The Overall Dining Experience

It is very important to continually perceive things from the guests' point of view. It is easy to take things for granted when one works in a restaurant every day. You can become oblivious to the servers' eating at a wait station within view of the guests, or the lovely display shelf at the entrance being used to hold ketchups, or a hundred other things. It is important to every foodservice operation to develop a system for regularly eliciting comments from guests on their dining experience, evaluating the comments, and taking prompt action to correct problems the comments reveal.

Mystery Guests

Some restaurants have a mystery-guest program and either hire professional shoppers or ask regular guests to come in for a complimentary meal and evaluate the experience. You should prepare a detailed report for the evaluators to fill out covering service, decor, food, cleanliness, and so on. (Refer to Figure 10-2 for a sample form for this type of report.) An evaluation should be done as frequently as possible, and at least once a week. The staff should be familiar with the report, so they know the standards expected of them. A variety of mystery guests should be rotated so no one party comes in often enough to be recognized by the staff.

You need not use professional shoppers. There are probably many people in your area who can be trained to be evaluators for you and who will do an excellent job. Ten to fifteen couples can be selected for this program. The couples should be people who eat out a great deal, are used to dining in similar restaurants, and who are intelligent and trustworthy. The couples should understand the purpose of the program and not be so flattered at receiving a complimentary meal that they will feel obliged to give you excellent ratings. The people chosen should also take an interest in evaluating your restaurant, pay attention to details, and write many useful comments on the form instead of just answering yes or no to all the questions. One couple a week should be scheduled to evaluate the restaurant.

There are several reasons for using couples instead of single diners. Couples will be easier to get, since no one enjoys dining out alone. Couples will also be able to sample more of your food and check both restrooms. They probably will not arouse as much suspicion as people dining alone. (You do need to keep their identity from the staff, who will be quite clever in trying to figure out who your mystery guests are.) It is preferable to use married couples over single men and women, because entertaining a date is not conducive to doing a good job of evaluating the restaurant. Of course, for business lunches, you will have to find someone to dine alone or bring a co-worker.

Payment for the evaluators is usually a free meal for two, with the evaluators leaving their own gratuity. The method of payment should not arouse suspicion. If a gift certificate would tip the servers off that the guests are evaluators, the manager will not be able to use the couple for very many visits. In this case, the evaluators should pay by cash or credit card and be reimbursed afterwards by the restaurant.

The evaluators should make many valuable, factual comments. If the evaluators' comments do not specifically describe facts, the couple should not be used again. For example, a comment such as, "The hostess did not look up from her notes when we walked in," specifically describes what the hostess did and is a very helpful comment. If the evaluators merely say, "The hostess made us feel unwelcome," then they are giving their emotional reaction without indicating the facts that gave rise to it. Comments like this are not helpful, because they fail to identify the action that needs to be corrected.

The stipulation should be that the evaluators fill out the form within 24 hours of their visit and mail it to you. If the evaluators fail to fill out the form promptly, they should not be used again, because many details will be forgotten if the form is not filled out immediately.

The evaluators should come and go without anyone knowing their identity, unless the manager who recommended them is present, or unless the manager wishes to seat the couple on a particular server's station. If a specific server needs to be evaluated, the manager on duty and the evaluators should arrange in advance for a specific day and time of the visit and a signal to tip off the manager that they are the evaluators. Many owners prefer that the evaluators be anonymous to everyone, including themselves and their managers.

Carefully review each evaluation. The servers and other employees involved should be shown the report and either praised or criticized for their efforts. Problems in the kitchen should be discussed, such as "The garlic bread was too bland," "The ice cream was too soft," or "The rolls were stale."

A program like this can be linked to a reward for the server or other staff members who get excellent ratings. In one restaurant, servers who achieve an excellent rating from the evaluators are awarded a dinner for two in another restaurant in the chain and are asked to fill out the same report on their dining experience. In this way, the award is also further training for them and a source of valuable information for the restaurant. In a fast-food restaurant, cashiers who get a perfect score on a shopper's report are given $10.

Review the report with employees who do not get a favorable evaluation. These employees should be evaluated again after they have had a chance to take corrective action to see if their performance has improved.

This kind of program is inexpensive to institute and can be invaluable to you. One such quality assurance program is given in Figures 10-1 and 10-2, which show the instructions to the evaluators and the form they fill out, respectively. These materials were custom-designed for Simms Landing, Marina Landing and H. Brinker's, some of the most popular restaurants in Denver, where the mystery-guest program is used.

Comment Cards

Guest comment cards are another source of information on service. The drawback is that many guests do not want to be bothered filling them out. Another limitation is that they really belong in informal restaurants and fast-food establishments. A comment card looks tacky on the table of a fine

(Text continued on p. 163)

Figure 10-1. Instructions for quality assurance evaluators. (Courtesy of Hospitality Industry Training, Inc.)

Today's date _____
Names of evaluators _____
Date and time of visit _____
Special instructions _____

Thank you for agreeing to be quality assurance evaluators. The purpose of our quality assurance program is to monitor our food, service, and atmosphere to be sure our guests are having the best dining experience we can provide.

Enclosed is the Quality Assurance Evaluation Form which we ask you to read prior to your visit, and complete and mail to us within 24 hours after your visit. Also enclosed is the gift certificate which will pay for food and beverages for two people. (We do ask if you would kindly leave the server a gratuity.)

Here are some suggestions for your visit:

• We ask you to visit the lounge, as well as the dining room. Please order cocktails, appetizers, dinner, wine, and dessert. We prefer that you order different things to eat, so you will be sampling more of the food.

• Ask to have your cocktail tab transferred from the bar to your dinner tab. The cocktail server should do this without question. This is so you will not have to show your gift certificate before the end of the meal. It may arouse suspicion. (We would like to keep your identities a secret as long as possible, so we can use you repeatedly.)

• Try to find out your cocktail server's, dinner server's, and busperson's name without arousing suspicion. Many servers will introduce themselves, although we do not insist upon it. If you absolutely cannot find out the name, please describe the employee. (We want to reward those employees who do an outstanding job and also correct the performance of those who do not meet our standards.)

• Give the server every opportunity to suggest drinks, wine, appetizers, and dessert before ordering these items. We want to evaluate the server's suggestive selling skills. We do not want the server to say something like, "Would you like an appetizer?" but rather to inform you of some of the specific appetizers we have. We are looking for specific suggestions that are tasteful and appropriate.

• Ask the server questions. For example, you might ask a cocktail server to describe a dry white wine we serve by the glass, or a dinner server to describe some items on the menu. We think that knowledge of the menu and wines is one of the most important aspects of service.

• Ask the server to suggest a wine that would go well with your dinner.

• Please visit *both* restrooms. (But not at the same time, as our staff will think you have "skipped out.")

• We are very concerned about the attitude of our staff. We want them to be friendly and enthusiastic and to enhance your dining pleasure. "Nice" isn't good enough— our staff needs to extend that extra hospitality that will make your visit memorable.

• We chose you because of your knowledge of restaurants and your judgment. We believe you will be fair in your judgments, neither nit-picky nor too easy.

• In order to pay for the meal, give the dinner server your gift certificate after he or she has presented the check. This certificate should be honored for your full meal, including cocktails in the lounge. If there should be any problem, ask for a manager and identify yourself. Otherwise you should come and go without anyone, even the managers, knowing who you are.

• **Please fill in the form within 24 hours after your visit to assure that the experience is fresh in your mind,** and mail it to the general manager. We encourage you to take notes discreetly during your visit on a small pad and not let the servers see the form.

Again, thank you very much for assisting us. We look forward to your frank and candid comments.

Figure 10-2. Quality assurance evaluation form. (Courtesy of Simms Landing.)

EXTERIOR

Did you find adequate parking? _____

If you used the valet parking, was the attendant courteous and efficient? _____

Were the parking lot and exterior grounds clean? _____
_____

If it was snowing or raining, were the steps slippery? _____
_____

Any other comments, positive or negative, about the exterior? _____
_____

LOBBY/HOSTESS

Was the lobby clean and the decor appealing? _____

Were you greeted promptly by a hostess? _____

Was she neat, clean, and well groomed? _____

Was the hostess (circle one):
perfunctory   polite but reserved   very warm and friendly

Were employees socializing around the hostess station? _____

Were you promptly shown to a table or directed to the lounge? _____

If shown to a dining room table, how well did the hostess seat you? Did she walk
with you, assist you in seating, and tell you to enjoy your meal? _____

If there was a wait, were you told approximately how long it would be and did the
estimate turn out to be fairly accurate? _____

If the restaurant was crowded, were you guided by a hostess on how to find a seat in
the lounge? _____

THE LOUNGE

Bartender

If you sat at the bar, evaluate the bartender. Was he or she well groomed, friendly,
prompt, and were the drinks good? _____
_____
_____

How was the service of the other bartenders?

_____

Cocktail Server

What was your cocktail server's name? _____

If you sat at a table, evaluate the cocktail server. Was he or she well groomed and friendly? Was the service prompt? Did the server get your order right and was it served without asking who gets what item?

_____
_____
_____

Did the server suggest refills on cocktails when your drinks were almost empty?

_____

Did the server suggest appetizers? Did he or she do a good job of trying to sell you appetizers? Were specific appetizers mentioned to entice you? _____

_____

Did the server do a good job of trying to keep your table neat? _____

What did you have to eat and drink, and how did it taste? _____
_____
_____

How were the other cocktail servers? Did they appear to be well groomed, friendly, and competent?

_____

Were you notified when your table was ready and escorted to the table? Was the hostess gracious? _____

Any other comments on the cocktail service?

_____
_____

THE DINING ROOM

The Decor and Atmosphere

Was the room neat, clean, and attractive looking? Was the floor free of papers and debris? _____

_____

The Table

Were your table and chairs clean and free of crumbs? _____

Figure 10-2. *(continued)*

Was the table set correctly, with napkins, silverware, wine glasses, butter plates, wine menu, salt, pepper, sugar caddy, ashtray, matches, and flowers? _____

Was the silverware clean? _____

Were the glasses free of smudges and fingerprints? _____

The Server

Your server greeted you in _____ minutes.

What was your server's name? _____

Describe the server's appearance. _____

Were you greeted promptly and courteously? _____

Was the server friendly, enthusiastic, and helpful? _____

Did the server show good technical skills? For example, was your order served without asking who gets what? Was the order correct? Was the lady served first?

Did the server show good suggestive selling skills? For example, did he or she mention specific items and describe them in an appealing way? Were the suggestions appropriate? _____

Were the following items suggested to you by the server:
Cocktails? _____
Appetizers? _____
Wine? _____
Dessert? _____
An after-dinner drink or specialty coffee? _____
Other (please specify) _____

Did the server show good knowledge of the menu? Was the server able to answer your questions? _____

Did the server show good knowledge of the wines, pronouncing their names correctly, describing them, and making suitable recommendations to accompany your meal? _____

Was the wine served correctly? _____

Was the rate of service suitable to your needs—neither rushed nor slow? _____

What was the busperson's name? _____

Was the busperson well groomed, friendly, and attentive? Did the busperson do a good job clearing the table and refilling the water glasses? _____

Was the bread server well groomed, friendly, and attentive?

Describe the other service personnel you observed on other stations. Were they well groomed, friendly, and did they appear to be giving good service? _____

Were service personnel on their stations and attentive or were they socializing among themselves? _____

Any other comments on the service? _____

The Food

What did you eat? Describe its appearance and taste. Did you enjoy the food? Was hot food served hot?

Appetizers _____

Main course _____

Desserts _____

Bread/muffins _____

Figure 10-2. *(continued)*

What did you have to drink? How did it taste? Describe cocktails, wine, coffee, specialty coffees, etc.

_____

_____

Was everything you ordered rung up on the check? _____

Did you notice a manager on the floor and, if so, what was he or she doing?

_____

Did the hostess or any other employee bid you goodbye on your way out?

_____

THE RESTROOMS

Were the restrooms clean and amply stocked with toilet tissue, paper towels, and soap. Were they neat? _____

_____

OVERALL EXPERIENCE

Give the restaurant a rating of A (excellent), B (good), C (average), or F (fails) in each of the following categories:

Cocktail Lounge Service _____   Dining Room Service _____
Food _____   Decor _____   Overall _____

Indicate any additional comments you have about any aspect of your dining experience.

_____

_____

Thank you for your evaluation. We appreciate your assistance in our quality assurance program.

NAMES OF DINERS _____
PHONE NUMBER _____ DATE AND TIME OF VISIT _____
Please mail completed form to: _____

_____

_____

_____

dining establishment. However, within the context of an informal restaurant, comment cards can be a very valuable measure of service if they are easy to fill out and if guests are prompted to fill them out. One franchisee of 20 fast-food restaurants computerizes the responses he receives and gives out awards monthly to the entire staff of the restaurant that has the most number of favorable comments for the month. The awards may be tickets to a rock concert or food items, for example. In these restaurants, the staff encourages guests to fill out the cards so the percentage of guest responses is high. In another fast-food chain, pencils are placed on each table near the comment card, making it convenient for guests to respond.

Manager's Talks with Guests

It is always impressive when the manager takes the time to walk around the dining room and talk to the guests. Patrons feel that the manager really cares about the business. And a tableside visit from the chef, who comes into the dining room wearing a (clean) uniform and tall hat, can really gain the guests' favor. How can guests feel more pampered and well cared for than when the chef or manager makes a special trip to the table to inquire about their meals? If the proprietor asks earnestly, many guests will speak frankly about their dining experience. If the operator does not get defensive and start making excuses, but accepts criticism gratefully, many guests will feel free to give negative comments because they will like him or her and want to help improve the restaurant. (This practice may also be considered as one of the informal means of monitoring performance. It becomes more formalized when the manager makes a regular practice of it, takes notes on the guests' comments, and follows up with employees to take corrective action.)

Hostess Questionnaire

A similar strategy, and one that works in a more formal restaurant where comment cards are inappropriate, is the hostess questionnaire. A very attractive and personable hostess (or host) walks around the dining room and approaches guests' tables while they are having coffee. She may offer a complimentary after-dinner drink or dessert (if none are on the table) to the guests if they would be so kind as to answer a few questions about their dining experience. The questions should not take more than a few minutes of the guests' time. They should cover food, service, decor, and any other comments the guests care to make. The hostess should thank the guests warmly for their assistance. The comments should be tallied, preferably using a computer. Restaurants needing improvement in their scores should set goals for higher ratings from the guests. If this questionnaire is done two or three nights a week, sampling approximately 20 parties per night, you will get a very good indication of your guests' reactions to your restaurant and of how to better please them.

Other Ideas

An institutional feeder gave guests chips to toss into one of five barrels by the cafeteria's exit. Each barrel had a face drawn on it showing different degrees of satisfaction from a frown to a wide grin. Each guest was asked to toss the chip in the barrel that reflected his or her opinion of the food. The managers set goals to improve the food and, over a period of time, met the goals. The guest responses gave them the information they needed to set their goals and measure their improvement.

A coupon could also be given to the guest with instructions to "give this coupon to an employee who does something exceptionally nice for you." This idea worked very successfully at an amusement park. In this case the customers are setting the standards for what they consider exceptionally nice service and the employees' performance is being measured by the number of coupons they collect. Rewards can be offered to employees who accumulate a certain number of coupons. Care must be taken to insure that the employees do not have access to any coupons except those given to them by the guests.

Sales

Sales are easier to monitor than service, especially with the computerized systems available today. It is almost futile to judge sales as a group effort among all servers, because individual sales can vary significantly among servers. Sales should be measured per individual server. In order to properly analyze individual sales of servers, a computerized system becomes very desirable. The following are some pitfalls to avoid in monitoring server sales.

Pitfall #1: Measuring One Parameter Only

Measuring the sales of only one item is a popular thing to do. For example, consider the popular practice of measuring wine sales. The server with the highest wine sales wins a contest. The problem with this approach is that some servers will improve in wine sales while their sales of other liquor items will drop, resulting in no actual gain in total alcoholic-beverage sales for the restaurant.

One restaurant that ran a wine contest found that its wine sales increased by exactly the same number of cents per customer as its sales of other liquor decreased. The winner of the contest had the highest wine sales, but her sales of other liquor decreased markedly. She said that occurred because she stopped suggesting cocktails and only suggested wine. Other servers who increased their wine sales without dropping their sales of other liquor actually had higher total sales of alcoholic beverages than did the winner of the contest, which made them more worthy of an award than was the winner of the wine contest.

It is more reasonable to measure total alcoholic-beverage sales per customer than it is to single out any one area of alcoholic beverage. It may be worthwhile to emphasize one product over another if that product has a higher profit margin or if the manager wants the servers to get accustomed to suggesting it. However, as a general practice, singling out one item can cause an increase in its sale, but often at the expense of the sale of other items, resulting in no net gain in sales for the restaurant.

The same thing occurs with dessert and appetizer sales. If there is a dessert contest, servers may actively discourage the guests from ordering appetizers in an effort to sell more dessert. A good way to avoid these problems is to monitor a server's total of wine, liquor, appetizer, and dessert sales per customer, and not single out any one category. It is the combined sales of all of these side items that really counts.

Pitfall #2: Measuring Sales Without Regard for the Number of Guests Served

A good computerized sales analysis program should be able to tell a restaurateur how a server's sales vary with the number of customers served. Sometimes there will be a general trend in the restaurant of sales per guest decreasing as number of guests increases. (The servers get too busy to suggest extras when there is high volume.) This information should be considered when determining station sizes that maximize sales and when comparing the sales of different servers. For example, if someone who served an average of 20 guests per shift gets higher sales per guest than another server who averaged 30 guests per shift, it does not necessarily follow that the former has a better sales record than the latter.

It can be difficult to permanently raise the average check. A short-term contest may bring a temporary increase, but then the average check has a tendency to return to precontest levels. Suggestive selling takes thought and practice, and despite the money motivation and the training, many servers do not make the effort necessary to change their habitual patterns at the table unless they are, in effect, forced to do so by the management. This can be accomplished with an effective and ongoing program for monitoring sales, along with setting goals for improvement where it is needed and regular discussions with individual servers to followup on their sales.

Daily sales figures easily become unmanageable if they are not compiled. Furthermore, daily figures are subject to chance variations. It is better to post and to analyze weekly or biweekly sales totals. This data should indicate the servers' check average, along with wine, other liquor, appetizer, and dessert sales per guest, and their total add-on sales, that is, the sum of their wine, liquor, appetizer, and dessert sales per guest excluding the entree. The total add-on sales figure is helpful in judging their suggestive selling abilities. Goals may be set on this figure, then the individual wine, liquor, appetizer, and dessert sales should be analyzed to find the areas of weakness and strength.

This data should also be computed for a longer period, such as every two months, for each server. The two-month figures should be the basis of the manager's individual conferences with the servers to review their sales, determine whether they met their goals, and set goals for the next period. Setting goals with the servers means that the manager and server should come up with reasonable ideas for suggesting things at the table. The server should agree to trying some of these ideas for the next two-month period. The manager should make notes of the server's commitments and follow up after two more months.

It is good to establish a baseline for sales before any training or incentive programs are begun. This baseline may be for a two-month period. Then the manager can judge the effects of the training and incentive efforts on the sales.

The goal should be to raise the restaurant's average sales by a certain percentage. The servers who exceed the goal should be recognized for their achievement and encouraged to continue their fine performance.

Individuals with chronically poor sales may eventually need to be replaced, because maintaining a certain sales level should be part of the job requirements. When newcomers are hired, they should be told that sales are a part of their job and that they will be expected, after a sufficient training period, to maintain certain sales.

It also is necessary to regularly reemphasize to the servers that they should always be suggesting items for the guests' pleasure. In addition, one should stress that alcohol is not to be served to minors or to intoxicated persons. It is very important to monitor service along with sales to be sure that the servers' suggestions are tasteful and enhance the guests' pleasure. You do not want to raise the average check by the servers' using high-pressure sales techniques and offending guests. Always keep in mind that the average sales per guest are very important, but service and guest satisfaction is what will build volume, which is even more important. So, the program to monitor sales must always be part of an overall effort to improve guest satisfaction. The servers should fully understand this and be ineligible for awards if there have been guest complaints or problems with their service.

Sales contests can be run weekly and results posted. Points can be accrued in weekly contests toward a prize of greater value. A thorough sales analysis can be done every two months with each server on an individual basis. With this formula, I have achieved significant and lasting increases in the average check.

Food

Guest reaction to the food can be monitored through the mystery-guest program and through you or the host or hostess talking to the guests. Customer's reaction to the food can also be elicited through comment cards. Comments should relate to the menu offerings, the taste of the food, the size of the portions, the appearance and temperature of the food, and the price. For informal restaurants, guests might be asked to toss a coin into a barrel to register their opinion of the food, as described previously. Training on how to improve the quality of the food, combined with an incentive plan to award cooks for improving the customers' reactions to the food can be an effective way of monitoring and improving food quality. Specific programs can also be developed to reward the kitchen staff for low food costs, such as a bonus for any period in which the food cost falls below a certain percentage.

Attendance/Punctuality

Some restaurants offer a bonus to employees for excellent attendance and/or punctuality. Some managers present the bonus as a "pay increase" that is given on the last day of a three-month period and retroactive to the first day of the period. The increase is contingent upon the employee meeting the attendance and punctuality standards set by the manager. The bonus might be $.25 per hour and the goal might be 100% attendance for the period. The pay increase is not a permanent one, but must be earned each quarter.

Cleanliness

Problems with cleaning can often be avoided by preparing a thorough checklist of what has to be cleaned and by assuring that employees carefully follow the checklist prior to their going off shift.

Consider the following example: A new manager had a terrible problem which she inherited from the former manager. The tables were not being set up properly by the closing servers at the end of the evening shift. The opening servers were not scheduled time to set up stations because this was supposed to be done by the night shift. The opening servers would get busy soon after the restaurant opened. They would find themselves running for utensils that were not on the tables, or salt shakers would be greasy, or there would be crumbs on the chairs.

The new manager decided to put an end to all this. She posted a notice reminding the night servers that it was their responsibility to set the tables. She also posted a detailed procedure explaining exactly how the tables were to be cleaned and set up. She had a meeting with the servers and showed them how she wanted the tables set up. In other words, she clearly set the standards and communicated them to the servers.

Next, she developed a means of measuring the servers' performance. Every station was to be carefully checked by the closing manager each night before the server was allowed to punch out. And there was immediate feedback. If the tables were set properly, the server could go home, but if one table was unsatisfactory, the server would have to strip all the tables and repeat the entire cleaning procedure.

This system for monitoring performance permanently solved the problem. The manager did not have to check every table each evening. It eventually became a spot-check of a few servers, although some checking was done each night. As a result of instituting this system, there no longer was a problem of dirty tables. Other kinds of cleaning problems can be handled similarly.

In an effort to interject an element of fun into cleaning, some managers have hidden dollar bills in out-of-the-way areas. An employee would have to clean very thoroughly to discover them. Other managers have hidden colored dots that are removable and self-adhesive. An employee who finds a dot posts it next to his or her name on a wall chart. There is an award for the employee who fills his or her row on the chart with dots.

Appearance

The premeal muster was already mentioned as a means of checking appearance. Premeal meetings are also excellent methods of communicating with the staff on a daily basis regarding all aspects of their work. When servers do not all start at the same time, it still may be possible to hold the premeal meeting when all have arrived and the restaurant is still not busy. One server may have to stay on the floor while the others meet.

Premeal meetings are an excellent way of communicating with the kitchen staff, as well. They need not last longer than ten minutes, yet having them regularly is like having a one-hour meeting with the staff each week—a lot can be accomplished through these short daily meetings.

If a premeal meeting is absolutely impossible, another method will have to be used for checking appearance. An appearance spot-check can be effective if you adhere to it. The names of the entire front-of-the-house staff are listed on a sheet of paper. Next to their names are columns that represent two-week periods. Your job is to single out each employee sometime within the two-week period and check that person's appearance. If it is completely satisfactory, the employee gets an A rating. It if falls short, he or she gets a lower rating with a notation of the problem made on the sheet. Employees who consistently get A's on their appearance spot-check may be eligible for an award or for points toward an award. The spot-check also gives the manager a record of those employees who consistently fail to meet appearance standards. These employees will need to show improvement or be subject to disciplinary procedures.

Try some of these ideas and devise your own, as well, to monitor employee performance. Sometimes one has to try a few ideas and refine them before a system is found that is effective. It is always a good idea to start a program on a small scale for a trial period and see how it works before committing oneself to it long-range.

The Role of Meetings in Maintaining Performance Standards

There is a need for ongoing communication with the staff. Employees need to be regularly reminded of the importance of their work to the success of the business and of the importance of hospitality to guests. Problems and conflicts need to be aired and resolved.

There is a great value in devising a means of regularly communicating with employees at a time when you and your employees are not "operational." When you and your staff are not waiting on customers, preparing orders, and washing dishes, you can all pay attention to the subject at hand, listen, think, develop points, consider plans, and, in short, communicate with each other. This cannot be done on the run. The various departments in the restaurant benefit greatly from having regular meetings, perhaps for just one hour once a month, for the purpose of discussing the state of the business, problems within the department, and plans for their resolution.

The following is a suggested structure for regular communication meetings with the staff.

The State of the Business

In order to get employees to care about the business, you must first see to it that they understand it. Many employees think that the financial pie graph of the restaurant consists of a tiny 5% wedge that represents expenses, and a huge 95% wedge that represents the owner's profit. They will be more concerned about food cost, sales, breakage, and everything else that matters if they understand the nature of these problems and their effects on the business. This is why the first five or ten minutes of the meeting may be spent informing employees of the state of the business. Suggested points to cover include sales (are they low or high?), customer counts (are they off?), new menu items, reports of mystery guests, responses on customer comment cards, special promotions, personnel changes, labor costs, and so on. This is also an excellent time to praise any employees who have done an exceptional job and award those who have earned incentive gifts.

The Main Point of the Meeting

The bulk of the time of the communication meeting generally is spent on some point that represents a problem for the department that needs to be resolved. It might be an area where retraining or additional training is needed, such as a menu class, wine class, review of service, cooking pointers on some items on the menu, sanitation class, review of cleaning procedures, review of appearance and attendance standards, and so forth. A film might be shown or an outside speaker brought in to cover the particular topic. This part of the meeting can also include demonstration of techniques, such as how to seat guests, and practice of the technique by the staff.

Employees' Comments

While employees are free to make comments throughout the meeting on the topics being discussed, at the end of the meeting they are given an opportunity to air any problems, concerns, or suggestions they might have about any aspect of their jobs. You might even go around the room and call on each employee to ask for comments. Encourage the employees to speak. They should not be ridiculed or criticized for their comments. Although you may not agree with everything the employee says, you need to respectfully address that person's concerns if you are to establish a climate for a free exchange of views.

Consider the following example from one communication meeting of how a manager handles an employee suggestion with which she does not agree:

Employee: "Why don't we take the hamburgers and salad entrees off the dinner menu, so the guests who come in will spend more and boost sales. We have a long wait anyway, and many people leave because they don't want to wait, so why don't we be sure to keep the ones that want to spend money?"

Manager: "I understand what you're saying, but I can tell you that when that idea was tried in our other restaurant, it did not work out the way you say. What it did was almost completely eliminate the early evening and late night traffic. Business was off from five to seven o'clock and again after ten. That's why I'm not willing to try it here. I think it's already been tried and did not work as we would have liked it to."

Here the manager respects the employee's point of view and gives her reason for holding the opposite point of view. Regardless of whether you will agree with them or not, employees should feel free to voice their problems and suggestions and know that they will get a fair hearing.

The meeting may close with several points that require follow-up. For example, if there is a shortage of spoons, you may agree to circulate more spoons while the employees agree to load and unload the bus trays more carefully to avoid loss of silverware. Someone in the group should take minutes of the meeting, and you should follow up at the next meeting on any actions that were to be taken by you and the group.

Refer to Figure 10-3 for a suggested format for your communication meetings. This format is reprinted with the permission of Inhilco, Inc. It is also used by its parent company, Hilton International.

The Role of Performance Appraisals in Maintaining Performance Standards

Performance appraisals are periodic reviews of the employee's overall performance. A manager prepares for a performance appraisal by evaluating the employee's performance, usually with the aid of a particular form that is used for that purpose; then the two have a meeting to discuss the employee's performance. The purpose of performance appraisals is to maintain good performance and to improve poor performance. (Typically these reviews are done once every six months to once a year; but a case can be made for doing them more frequently.)

Performance appraisals serve a purpose that is not served by daily feedback, be it praise or criticism. Performance appraisals focus on the employee's entire performance and not merely on any one aspect of it. Daily feedback focuses on one particular aspect of performance, such as appearance, sales, or punctuality.

Figure 10-3. Monthly communication meeting agenda. (Courtesy of Inhilco, Inc.)

I. STATE OF THE BUSINESS
(Sales, customer counts, new menu items, personnel changes, new promotions, etc.)

II. POINTS TO COVER
(Policies not carried out properly, review of training in certain areas, attendance/punctuality, appearance, guest relations, preparation and service of food, sales figures, etc.)

III. EMPLOYEES' INPUT
(Ask for comments, suggestions, complaints, problems, etc. Go around the room to each employee and give him or her a chance to speak.)

Both you and your employees need an understanding of their overall performance, an understanding that daily feedback cannot give. This is the purpose of doing periodic performance appraisals. Appraisals can help promote good work habits, indicate areas where additional training is needed, keep performance up to standards, and aid the deserving employee in advancing within the company.

How does one appraise performance? The performance appraisal process consists of the following steps:

1. Establish standards of good performance.

2. Evaluate the employee's performance versus the standards.

3. Communicate the evaluation and discuss performance with the employee.

The steps are exactly parallel to those used in maintaining performance standards in general (i.e., set standards and goals, measure performance, and give feedback), except that in a performance appraisal the entire performance is being judged and not just one aspect of it.

Establish Standards of Good Performance

Standards should have been established during the training process. The job checklists given in Chapter 4 explain what tasks the employee is required to do. The training manual indicates how the employee should perform the various tasks of the job. The manual is the book of standards, and the employee should be judged by how his or her performance compares to that specified in the training manual.

Evaluate the Employee's Performance versus the Standards

It can be very difficult to be objective in evaluating performance. Employees may behave one way when you are around and another way when you are absent, so you do not always get a complete picture of the employee's performance. Or, you may have certain biases that cause you to underrate or overrate the employee. For all of these reasons and more, you need to make a scrupulous effort to be fair in your evaluations. Sometimes a manager will ask assistants and supervisors to also evaluate the employee, so there is more than one point of view. Then the managers can discuss their evaluations and arrive at one that is, presumably, more equitable.

A form needs to be used for appraising an employee's performance. The form is like a report card, indicating how the employee rates in all key areas of the job. The form may include (1) traits that are essential to the job, such as reliability, cooperation, and initiative; (2) actions the employee takes to perform the job, such as frying food, stacking the bus trays, and taking the customer's order; and (3) outcomes, or results, of the employee's actions, such as sales per customer, number of favorable customer comments, or average time taken to prepare orders.

The sample job checklists for servers and cashiers given in Chapter 4 are designed to be used for appraising performance as well as for training. They primarily measure actions, or how well the employee performs the required tasks. The server form also measures an outcome, sales, and asks for the employee's average sales per guest. Another performance evaluation form is given in Figure 10-4. This form also focuses primarily on the employee's actions and is specific for a particular position, that of the broiler cook.

Figure 10-4. Performance evaluation—broiler cook. (Courtesy of Mr. Steak, Inc.)

PERFORMANCE EVALUATION — BROILER COOK

ACTION

60 +   Acceptable
45-59 Review within 90 days
       for improvement
0-44   Review within 10 days
       for disciplinary action.

Staff Member's Name _____

Date of Evaluation _____

ACHIEVEMENT
Outstanding - 5 - Excellent
          Good - 4 - Above Average
Satisfactory - 3 - Average
      Minimum - 2 - Fair
Unsatisfactory - 1 - Poor

1. **APPEARANCE**   1 - 2 - 3 - 4 - 5
   Is neat, clean and well-groomed. Reports to work in clean
   appropriate uniform. Nails are clean and manicured. Hair
   is restrained, if long.

2. **GUEST AWARENESS**   1 - 2 - 3 - 4 - 5
   Is courteous, friendly and helpful to Guests. Anticipates the
   Guest's needs and satisfies them.

3. **COMMUNICATION**   1 - 2 - 3 - 4 - 5
   Communicates clearly and respectfully with other Staff
   Members and with Management, using proper terminology
   and/or vocabulary.

4. **RELIABILITY**   1 - 2 - 3 - 4 - 5
   Has good attendance and reports to work on time.

5. **COOPERATION**   1 - 2 - 3 - 4 - 5
   Willingly gives assistance by doing work other than his or
   her own to assist other Staff Members and Management.

6. **HANDLING PRESSURE**   1 - 2 - 3 - 4 - 5
   Can handle peak volume periods. Works quickly, concentrates
   on tasks at hand, and remains calm.

7. **OPENING/CLOSING/4:00 P.M. PROCEDURES/**
   WEEKLY SANITATION DUTIES   1 - 2 - 3 - 4 - 5
   Performs those duties assigned by checklists on a timely basis.
   Is careful and thorough in completing assigned tasks.

8. **BROILING STEAKS**   1 - 2 - 3 - 4 - 5
   Broils steaks according to the rotation broiling method. Obtains
   the proper score marks on the steaks, positions them correctly
   on the broiler, cooks them to the proper degree of doneness;
   can judge proper cooking of steaks by their color, firmness and
   position on the broiler. Has few returns. Keeps a burn chart.
   Cooks marinated items on a separate area of the broiler.

9. **READING GUEST CHECKS/COMMUNICATIONS**   1 - 2 - 3 - 4 - 5
Thoroughly reads Guest Checks. Knows the correct
abbreviations of all food items. Knows the number of each
child's plate. Communicates with Cooks and Waitpersons using
proper kitchen terminology. Understands the difference between
more fire and refire.

10. **COORDINATING ORDERS WITH FRY COOK
AND WAITPERSONS**   1 - 2 - 3 - 4 - 5
Properly and calmly directs Fry Cook to prepare menu items.
Calls the correct Waitpersons on the call system used in the
restaurant.

11. **PLATING PROCEDURES**   1 - 2 - 3 - 4 - 5
Knows the proper plate setups and accompaniments for all food
items. Places proper garnish on all plates. Attractively presents
finished appetizers/entrees to Waitpersons.

12. **CONSERVING ENERGY**   1 - 2 - 3 - 4 - 5
Follows the Energy Conservation Chart for times to turn
equipment on and off.

13. **FIRE SAFETY**   1 - 2 - 3 - 4 - 5
Is familiar with the correct operation of all fire safety systems,
and can locate and operate all fire extinguishers.

14. **STORING AND ROTATING FOOD**   1 - 2 - 3 - 4 - 5
Assists the Manager in receiving deliveries. Checks for quality
of items received; is alert to bulging cans, and boxes with blood
stains on them (indications of refrigerated or frozen foods left at
room temperature). Dates all food received and stores it at the
proper temperature. Stores food above 6″ from the floor. Stores
soaps and chemicals separate from food. Maintains clean,
organized storage areas.

15. **PORTION CONTROL/COST CONTROL**   1 - 2 - 3 - 4 - 5
Prepares and serves the correct portion sizes. Is conscious of
not wasting food. Wraps leftovers carefully. Stores food at the
proper temperature.

TOTAL POINTS_____

Evaluator's Comments _____

_____

Signature of Manager _____ Date _____

Staff Member's Comments _____

_____

Staff Member's Signature _____ Date _____

Rate the employee as excellent, good, needs improvement, or unsatisfactory (A, B, C, or F) in each important job category. You will need to have the facts to back up your evaluations, so the employee will understand the reasons for the rating. This may require that you keep written notes of specific instances of good and poor performance. Remember that good performance as well as poor needs to be included, and an overall evaluation of the employee needs to be arrived at.

Communicate the Evaluation and Discuss Performance with the Employee

The following are some important guidelines in conducting performance appraisals.

Let the Employee Speak

The performance interview should include a lot of employee participation. The employee should be encouraged to give evaluations and voice concerns.

Give Recognition

Acknowledge any aspects of the employee's performance that are praiseworthy.

Discuss Areas Where Improvement Is Needed

Of course, there is a tendency for employees to get defensive when discussing those touchy areas in which you want to see improvement. In order to minimize defensiveness, the discussion should be one in which two equals are trying to solve problems. It is wise not to flaunt your authority or in any way imply that the employee's shortcomings are a reflection on his or her character or intelligence. The rules for giving constructive criticism discussed in the next chapter should be followed. It is generally a good idea not to barrage the employee with too many areas for improvement. This approach is demoralizing, and it may in fact be impossible for the employee to improve in all areas at once. Select one or two key areas that will make a difference. At the next performance review, if there is improvement in those areas, then others can be addressed.

Set Goals for Improvement

Ask the employee to suggest ways to solve the problem. An employee who has proposed a course of action will be more committed to following it. Establish goals and gain the employee's commitment to try to achieve them. For example, if shoppers' reports show that the employee is not doing too much suggestive selling, and the individual's sales figures confirm this, then the employee has to make a commitment to do something differently at the table to boost sales.

Areas where the employee may need further training or plans to prepare the employee for a promotion to the next level (e.g., a busser to a server) may also be discussed during the performance review.

Agree on a Follow-up Date

You will not want to wait for the next performance review to check on whether the employee has improved. A date should be set to review those areas in which improvement is needed. Record this date on your calendar, find out if the improvement has occurred, and keep the date with the employee. Performance problems should not be allowed to slip, because they do not correct themselves.

In order for your training programs to be effective, it is crucial to monitor the performance of employees on a regular basis and to let them know how they are doing. Walking around the restaurant, setting up systems for monitoring performance, holding regular staff meetings, and conducting periodic performance appraisals are some effective ways of maintaining performance standards.

SUMMARY

In order to obtain lasting results from your training programs, you need to maintain performance standards on a regular basis after the training is completed. You must develop procedures to monitor the performance of your employees and communicate to them how they are doing.

You can monitor performance informally, by walking around the restaurant and watching employees work.

You can also develop formal systems for monitoring performance. Choose a particular aspect of the employee's job that is crucial to you. Then set goals or standards, measure the employee's performance against the standards, and give the employee feedback on how he or she is doing. Using this system, you can devise methods for monitoring service, sales, food quality, attendance and punctuality, cleanliness, appearance, and other aspects of performance.

Regularly scheduled staff meetings can be an invaluable way to communicate to the staff as a whole the state of the business and areas where improvement is needed. Staff meetings also give you an opportunity to hear the staff's comments and suggestions.

Periodic performance evaluations are important in evaluating the employee's overall performance, rather than just particular aspects of it. Here again, standards need to be set, the employee's performance judged versus the standards, and your evaluation communicated to the employee. The employee should be praised for good performance. Areas where improvement is needed should be discussed. Plans to improve should be agreed upon and a follow-up date set to see if the employee is making progress.

11

Human Relations Skills

In order to motivate employees and maintain performance standards, you must possess good skills at dealing with people.

Respecting the employee, praising, criticizing, and disciplining are some important human relations skills that you need on a daily basis in order to properly deal with your employees.

Respecting the Employee

First and foremost, you should respect your employees. This involves, for instance, being courteous to employees, politely asking them to do things, and making time to listen to the work-related problems that concern them. Respecting employees means giving them the benefit of a doubt. This does not imply that you will naively think the best of everyone, but that you will wait until you have the facts before drawing negative conclusions about the employee. Some managers instantly respond to any error by blaming an employee they think is deliberately doing the wrong thing. The respectful approach is to find out the relevant facts first, before you form your judgment. For example, if you see a cook wiping the kitchen counters with a linen napkin, find out the facts before screaming. Maybe the napkin has a hole in it and the cook figured it could not be used at the table, so he would use it for cleaning.

Praising

Praising is very important in both training and motivating employees. Praising trains employees by indicating to them that they have performed correctly. It is equally important for the employees to know what is correct as what is incorrect. Praising motivates employees because their good performance is recognized and appreciated. In this way, they are encouraged to continue the same good performance. Praising also motivates by building confidence in employees that they can handle the job.

Most managers need to make a conscious effort to praise, because they may feel embarrassed by complimenting an employee or worried that the employee will be embarrassed. The uncomfortable feeling many managers experience when praising does disappear with time as the manager gets more experienced at giving praise.

The most important rule about giving praise is that it should be sincere. Be genuine in your praise and convince the employee that you are sincere. It is often helpful to give the reasons for the praise, or to make the praise real with a specific incident, so the employee knows that it is genuine. Whenever possible, praise should be given publicly, such as at a staff meeting.

Here are some examples of praise:

You did an excellent job cooking tonight. Although we were very busy, you got the orders out quickly and there were no returns.

You do a very good job of selling wine. I notice that you suggest wine to your guests and help them make a selection. Your wine sales are high, which boosts your tips and our sales, as well.

Criticizing

Criticism is one of the most powerful tools you have for correcting poor performance. Criticism is beneficial to the employees, as well, because it improves their performance and builds their skills.

Some managers have difficulty criticizing because they are concerned that employees will dislike them for it. This is the chance one takes when giving criticism; you have to be willing to be disliked in order to do your job as manager. However, the criticism is likely to be accepted without resentment if it is given properly.

The following are some important guidelines for giving constructive criticism.

Criticize the Actions, Not the Person

Avoid flaunting your authority. Restrict your criticism to the actions, not the intelligence or character, of the employee.

Incorrect: "Don't you know that you shouldn't load bus trays like that? Common sense would tell you the glasses are going to break!"

(How could the employee not take offense at such an attack on his intelligence?)

Correct: "Don't stack those glasses like that, or they'll fall. Here's how to do it."

Criticize Important, Not Trivial, Things

If a waitress has made a superhuman effort to handle extra tables in a co-worker's absence, it is not the right time to complain to her about the top shelf of the condiment station being dusty.

You will lose your credibility with your employees if you always pick on relatively inconsequential things to criticize and miss the "big picture."

Be Clear

Clearly explain what the employee did incorrectly and what he should have done, instead.

Incorrect: "I'm sorry, but you just can't handle the lunch rush."

Correct: "I notice you're having difficulty getting into the kitchen on time to pick up your orders. Let's see how you can organize your time better. . . . "

Show Good Control of Anger

Anger is certainly justified when you have reason to believe that the employee had the knowledge to perform better, but willfully and without good reason performed incorrectly instead. Anger, however, should not be overused, because it provokes fear. Anger should not be used to vent your own frustrations on employees who have done nothing wrong, but who have the misfortune of being nearby when you are enraged over an entirely unrelated matter. For example, if your boss chews you out for something and you are angry, do not vent your feelings by screaming at your busser for a fork being crooked on the table.

Cushion the Criticism When This Is Justified

If there are understandable circumstances which could lead the employee to take the incorrect action, or if a significant part of the employee's perform-ance was correct, it is appropriate to indicate this in the criticism.

For example, "I know that with two small children, it is difficult to get to work at 9 A.M., but when you're late, the prep work doesn't get finished in time for lunch." Or, "Your wine service was very good, but you should twist the bottle after pouring to prevent drippage."

The understandable or positive aspect should only be indicated if it is justified, so the employee feels that you have seen the whole context. Certainly, an employee whose performance includes nothing laudable should not be misled into thinking he or she is doing a partially good job.

Use Humor to Ease the Tension

In cases in which the incorrect action is not too serious, a little humor can convey your message while assuring the employee that you are not overreacting.

For example, you may say to buspersons who are noisily loading the bus trays, "Think you guys can keep things down to a low roar?"

Disciplining

While the appeal to fear should be used sparingly, and the positive means of motivation tried first, it sometimes becomes necessary to inform the employee that his or her job is in jeopardy or to summarily dismiss that individual.

Discipline is required when a rule is broken that represents a major and inexcusable infraction of policies, such as stealing, taking drugs while at work, starting a fight with a co-worker, or being rude to a customer. In cases like these, constructive criticism is usually not appropriate, since the action is too obviously wrong to require an explanation, and the employee is often dismissed automatically. In order for the dismissal or other disciplinary action to be fair, employees should be told at the time of hire that certain actions are grounds for immediate discharge, and they should be given some examples of these kinds of actions. Employees should clearly understand in advance the consequences of certain actions, should they choose to take them.

Discipline is also necessary when a less serious rule is violated repeatedly. The one violation would not make discipline appropriate, but the repeated disregard for the rule makes discipline necessary. Examples of this include chronic lateness or absenteeism, failure to correctly portion items, or to clean one's station, or to follow virtually any instruction that has been given repeatedly. In cases like this, constructive criticism should be tried first to correct the problem, but if it is to no avail, disciplinary action is required.

Discipline Should Be Fair

The rules should be reasonable and the employees should know the rules. It is proper to take into account any extenuating circumstances, such as an employee's lateness being due to a snowstorm, which would excuse the infraction. In summary, the mistake must be a willful violation of a reasonable rule the employee clearly knows must be obeyed.

Discipline Should Be Administered in Stages

With the exception of cases in which immediate discharge is justified, as mentioned above, there should be stages of discipline during which time the employee is given an opportunity to correct the undesirable behavior while knowing that failure to take corrective action will ultimately lead to dismissal.

For example, an employee has a problem with lateness, and constructive criticism has not corrected it. The employee may be given a verbal warning. If the problem is still not corrected, a written warning may be given, followed by dismissal. Some managers will give two written warnings prior to dismissing the employee. There is some option in the stages chosen, but the employee should clearly know at each stage what will happen next if his or her performance is not corrected. Suspension or dismissal should not come as a surprise.

Every stage of discipline should be documented in the employee's personnel file.

You should avoid sudden rampages in which employees are given written warnings for actions you had tacitly tolerated for a long time previously. In one case, the manager had never criticized the servers for addition mistakes on their checks. Then one day he suddenly became enraged about this issue, and wrote warning notices to all servers whose additions were off by even one penny (about two-thirds of the staff). The employees perceived the manager's actions as erratic and they did not know what to expect from day to day.

The manager could have instead called a staff meeting to inform employees that there have been addition mistakes in the past that were not noted on their record, but from now on there was going to be a new policy. He could have forewarned his staff that he would begin to issue warnings to employees who make addition mistakes. In this way, the employees would have been informed of the change in policy prior to being disciplined.

Practicing good human relations skills will have a profoundly positive effect on the performance of your staff. Respecting the employee, praising, criticizing, and disciplining correctly are all important in maintaining performance standards.

SUMMARY

In order to motivate employees and maintain their performance standards, you need to possess good skills at dealing with people, such as respecting the employee, praising, criticizing, and disciplining.

Respecting the employee includes being courteous, listening to job-related concerns, and giving the employee the benefit of a doubt.

Praising is important in training and motivating the employee. Praise should be genuine and the employee should know what he or she has done to deserve it.

Some guidelines for giving constructive criticism are (1) criticize the actions, not the person; (2) criticize important, not trivial, things; (3) be clear; (4) show good control of anger; (5) cushion the criticism when this is justified; and (6) use humor to ease the tension.

Discipline is necessary when (1) a rule is broken that represents a major infraction of policies or (2) a less serious rule is violated repeatedly and constructive criticism has been tried, but to no avail. Discipline should be fair, administered in stages, and documented in the employee's personnel file.

12

*The Manager as a Role Model**

One of the most powerful means of motivating employees, and hence maintaining their performance standards, is through a manager's own conduct. By observing how you do your own work, the employee forms conclusions about the job, the guests, and other employees that can strongly influence his or her motivation and performance. The fact that you profoundly influence your employees is inescapable. The only question is: Will you be a good or a bad role model?

The following are some important ways in which your own behavior influences your employees.

Being Competent

The employee's degree of respect for you is influenced by how competent you are. Although a certain amount of calamity is inevitable in a restaurant, the employee quickly becomes disgusted if there are chronic problems, such as volume being forecasted inaccurately, causing under- or overstaffing; inadequate supplies and equipment; weekly work schedules being posted too late and changed too often; and other problems which suggest to the employee that you do not know what you are doing.

---

*This chapter is adapted from an article by the author which appeared in *Restaurant Business* magazine, June 10, 1986.

The manner in which you deal with all the types of situations mentioned in this chapter reveals the degree of competence with which you manage your operation.

Making Sound and Consistent Decisions

If your decisions are sound and the employees know that they are, the staff grows to respect you as being competent. This improves employee motivation, because people tend to work harder for managers they respect and admire. However, if your decisions are perceived as nonsensical or arbitrary, the employees begin to resent the rules imposed upon them and are disinclined to follow procedures.

For example, one manager received a complaint from a party because the waitress "rushed them through the meal." The party, which had entered the restaurant near the closing hour, claimed the waitress served the main course too quickly and placed the check on the table before they even had a chance to order dessert. When they asked for coffee, the waitress told them there wasn't any more. The manager, in an angry rage, fired the waitress on the spot.

This unsound, emotional decision caused enormous resentment among the staff, because they felt that the cook and the night manager, in turn, rushed them into getting customers out as quickly as possible. The rashness with which the manager acted, before finding out the waitress's side of the story or considering her satisfactory past record as grounds for a lesser disciplinary action, embittered and de-motivated the staff.

Decisions should also be consistent. One manager lost the respect of his staff for requiring them to follow a strict appearance code while allowing a personal friend of his, who was a member of the staff, to flagrantly break the rules without reprisal. In cases like this, the employees conclude that the rules must not be too important if the manager does not enforce them consistently. Individuals on the staff also feel it is unfair for the manager to pick on them and not on others.

Planning and Organizing the Work

An environment that is well organized is much easier and more enjoyable to work in than one that is chaotic and confusing. You can create a calm environment by carefully planning and organizing the work. Is there a place for everything? Are employees trained to perform their jobs competently? Is the food of good quality and handled properly? Employees need an organized environment to function at their best.

Taking One's Own Job Seriously

The manager who serves as the best role model is one who takes his or her own job seriously.

If you are conscientious about doing your own work and are regularly on the floor checking how the employees are performing, the employees get the impression that you take the work seriously. Managers who flirt with the staff, drink too much at the bar, or otherwise goof off give employees the impression that they show little interest in the operation. Why should the employees show interest if they feel that the manager does not care?

Being Enthusiastic

To show that you take the work seriously, you do not have to have a deathlike, grim attitude about everything. Rather, you should communicate to the employees that the work is important. You also need to show enthusiasm for the work, to ease the tension of the work environment and make the establishment an enjoyable place in which to be. Enthusiasm is infectious. If you feel a certain excitement for the work, enjoy dealing with the guests and staff, thrive on the fast pace, savor the food you serve, and love the restaurant business, you can inject your staff with that same feeling about the business.

The manager who can maintain an optimistic attitude and take constructive action despite the problems, frustrations, and calamities that occur can have a profoundly positive influence on the employees' attitudes about the job. One restaurant had an early morning fire that caused substantial damage. The manager summoned his staff to extraordinary efforts to clean up the debris. Inspired by the determination and optimism of their manager, the staff was able to open the restaurant for lunch that very day, serving a limited menu of cold sandwiches. This was an enormous accomplishment that created a feeling of pride among the staff. It could not have occurred if the manager had given up, projected that all was hopeless, and believed the day was lost. (Even the customers were impressed with the efforts of the manager and staff to keep the business running. Customers supported them through a tough period and endured a week of cold sandwiches until the manager could get the kitchen operational again. The day of the fire was celebrated each year thereafter by customers and staff as the day "the bar was lit and the customers were sober.")

Respecting the Guests

Your hospitality has to be genuine if your employees are to respect the guests and extend the best in courtesy and service. One manager would nag his employees to be courteous to the guests but, while in the kitchen, he would make snide remarks about when Mr. Smith is going to leave or about how cheap Mr. Jones is. Regardless of how some guests can try one's patience, it is wise to refrain from showing irritation or hostility toward the guests in front of the employees, because this behavior tacitly gives the staff permission to act in kind.

Respecting the Employees

As discussed in Chapter 11, it is important to treat employees with respect. This includes giving them the benefit of a doubt, paying attention to them when they speak to you, and giving orders courteously. For example, it is a bad practice to make negative remarks about some employees in the presence of others, because the others feel they are probably talked about negatively when they are not around.

Here is how one manager made a point of respecting his employees and acknowledging their efforts: He invited the higher-level managers in the company to his staff meetings. The manager used these opportunities to praise deserving employees for their outstanding performance. This exposure to upper management and the appreciation of their efforts motivated the employees to work even harder for the manager.

Respecting the Managers

Employees need to know that a general manager supports his or her assistant managers and supervisors. Your view of your management team affects the employees' view of and performance for those same managers. Be careful to avoid making snide remarks about your assistants in front of the employees. If you have a problem with any of your assistants, discuss it privately with the person. If you hold your managers in esteem, you will be communicating to the employees that they, too, should respect them.

While restaurant managers are usually on their best behavior in front of the guests, they sometimes drop their guard in the presence of their employees. When you are tired or angry about something, it is easy to show your worst side to your employees. This practice can have serious negative effects on the attitude and performance of your staff.

Remember that you are the most important role model that your employees have, and use the power of your own attitudes and actions to motivate your staff to greater achievement.

SUMMARY

One of the most powerful means of motivating employees and influencing their performance is through your own behavior. The following are some important ways in which you can serve as a positive role model to your employees: (1) being competent, (2) making sound and consistent decisions, (3) planning and organizing the work, (4) taking your own job seriously, (5) being enthusiastic, (6) respecting the guests, (7) respecting the employees, and (8) respecting the managers.

PART SEVEN

PERSONAL APPLICATION

13

Self-Analysis Exercise: How Well Do You Train Your Employees?

Answer the following questions honestly to determine how effective you are at training your employees.

1. Are you convinced that training is important?

2. Are you committed to spend time, money, and effort on training?

3. Do you have a system for training your staff and do you resist the temptation to leave training to chance?

4. Do you spend time orientating new employees to your operation?

5. Do you use an orientation checklist?

6. Do you have an up-to-date personnel handbook that you give to all new employees?

7. Do you follow up with new employees and their trainers to keep abreast of the trainees' progress during the first few weeks of employment?

8. Do you use training manuals and/or audiovisual programs to train employees?

9. Is there consistency between the procedures actually being used in the restaurant and those described in the manuals and audiovisual programs?

10. Do you use quizzes and performance evaluations to certify an employee to work a given position?

11. Do you carefully select your trainers?

12. Do you have a means of training your trainers?

13. Do you reward your trainers for their efforts?

14. Do you include some off-the-job instruction for new employees, as well as for veteran employees who need to improve their skills?

15. Do your trainers use a combination of explanation, demonstration, and practice when instructing?

16. Do you regularly walk aroung the restaurant talking to guests and watching employees at work?

17. Have you developed systems for monitoring performance in crucial areas, such as guest satisfaction, service, sales, food quality, food cost control, and cleanliness?

18. Do you offer incentives for outstanding performances?

19. Do you hold communication meetings with your staff on a regular basis, such as once a month?

20. Do you hold periodic performance evaluations with your staff?

21. Do you carefully plan your meetings and do they accomplish your objectives?

22. Do you treat your employees with respect?

23. Do you regularly praise employees who deserve it?

24. Do you criticize employees in private when they deserve it?

25. Do you criticize constructively, without attacking the person's character or intelligence?

26. Do employees know at the time of hire that certain actions may be subject to immediate dismissal?

27. With the exception of major infractions of the rules which are subject to immediate dismissal, do you discipline in stages?

28. Do you document your verbal and written warnings to your employees?

29. Are you a good role model to your employees?

30. Carefully evaluate your answers to the preceding questions and give yourself a rating on how effectively you train your staff and maintain their performance standards:

_____ A   Excellent

_____ B   Good, but improvement is possible

_____ C   A lot of improvement is needed

_____ F   Massive improvement is urgently needed on all counts

14

Exercise in Designing a Training Program

This exercise should be completed by the entire management team as a group in order to design an effective training program for the operation. Use additional paper where necessary to fully answer the questions.

Section 1: Orientation

Design an effective orientation program to familiarize a new employee with the restaurant.

1. Who will conduct orientation training for you?

2. Describe how it will be done.

3. When will the orientation training be done?

4. Will you use any of the following:

    ———————— an orientation checklist

    ———————— a personnel handbook

    ———————— follow-up meetings

    ———————— an audiovisual presentation

    ———————— other (specify)

5. Who will develop these materials for you, and when will they be completed?

6. Will you ask the new employee to sign any statements, such as the tip declaration policy, rules for service of alcoholic beverages, etc.? If so, list and describe these statements.

7. What are the costs of orientation training?

The remainder of this exercise will deal with job skills training. Select a position in your restaurant for which you need a training program. Once you have designed a training program for this position, you can use the same process to design training programs for all other positions in your operation.

The program is designed to train a new employee in the position. If you want to retrain the current staff, consider modifying the program to emphasize problem areas and consider using group instructional techniques.

The position is ——————————————————————————.

Section 2: The Job Breakdown

Break the job down into a series of tasks that will have to be learned by the new employee.

Section 3: Selecting a Trainer

1. Select a trainer (or trainers) for this position and give the reasons for your selection.

2. What will you ask the trainer to do?

3. How will you train the trainer?

4. What materials will you give the trainer to assist him or her?

5. How will you measure the trainer's effectiveness?

6. How will you reward the trainer for his or her efforts?

Section 4: Training Materials

1. Will you develop a training manual for the position?

2. Will you develop audiovisual materials or use any commercially available programs to assist in training?

3. Describe in detail how you will develop your custom-designed materials. Who will write the manual? How long will it take?

4. How will you evaluate the trainee? Will you use quizzes and performance evaluations?

Who will prepare these materials?

When will they be completed?

How and when will you use these materials in the training program?

Section 5: The Training Schedule

Design a training schedule for the new employee in the position you have chosen. Include on-the-job and off-the-job training. Describe the new employee's first few days or weeks on the job and indicate what he or she will be taught each day.

Section 6: Maintaining Performance Standards

1. Describe your plans for regularly measuring performance of the new employee as well as all employees in this position. What incentives will you offer for outstanding performance?

2. Will you hold premeal, postmeal, or lengthier communication meetings with all employees in this position? If so, who will conduct them and how often will they be held?

3. Will you conduct periodic performance evaluations with all new employees in this position? If so, who will conduct these evaluations and how often will they be done?

4. Describe your plans for training the management team in human relations skills and in being a good role model.

Section 7: Costs of Job Skills Training

1. Cost per trainee: What will be the cost of training a typical new person in the position you have chosen? Include the trainer's and trainee's time, the cost of materials used, and any bonus the trainer will receive.

2. One-time costs: What will be the costs of preparing and/or purchasing the training materials? Include the writer's fee for preparing the training manual, printing, audiovisual production, photography, and any other development costs.

APPENDIX

Sample Materials for Training Servers

*Appendix A: Rules of Service**

If you are enthusiastic about your work, courteous, and friendly and if you practice the rules of good service, your guests should have a pleasant and memorable dining experience. Be sure your busperson also follows the rules of good service as he or she assists you with service. It is important to communicate your needs to your busperson throughout service and to remember that *you are the busser's immediate supervisor.*

Prepare for Service
Check your Appearance

Clothes should be clean and ironed. Fingernails should be clean and manicured. If nail polish is worn, it should not be chipped.

Women should wear a white blouse with a black skirt hemmed below the knee, neutral stockings, and dark, conservative, comfortable shoes. Hair longer than shoulder length should be stylishly restrained. Jewelry and makeup should not be overstated.

Men should wear a white shirt, tie, and dark slacks, with dark socks and shoes. Beards are not allowed, and mustaches must be neatly trimmed. Men must be clean shaven. Hair should not extend below the nape of the neck.

Salespersons should all wear a clean, ribbed apron provided by the company.

Tennis shoes are not allowed.

---

*Courtesy of Marina Landing.

Check Your Station

- —Are tables and chairs clean and free of crumbs?
- —Has the busperson set the tables properly, with napkins, silverware, glasses, and bread plates? Take special care in checking glasses to be sure they are free of smudges.
- —Refill salt and pepper shakers, wipe them with a hot wet rag, then dry them.
- —Clean the wine menus, and replace soiled ones.
- —Clean and refill the sugar caddies, being sure you provide an ample supply of sugar and the two substitutes.
- —Place ashtray, matches, and flowers on the table.
- —Are tables aligned?
- —Are chairs pulled in close to tables?
- —Is the floor free of papers and other debris?

Check Your Sidestand

Be sure it is amply stocked with all the supplies you need. Unroll a few napkins and spot check silverware to be sure it has been wiped clean.

Know the Daily Specials

Be aware of the daily specials and soups *before* the start of service.

Seat the Guest

The hostess should have seated your guests graciously and given them menus.

Pour Water

You or your busperson should pour water for the guests. For large parties, try to pour the water before guests are seated, as this will greatly facilitate service.

The busperson should also greet the guests on his or her first trip to the table. For example, a busperson might simply say, "Good evening." This adds to the guests' feeling welcomed.

Greet the Guests and Take the Cocktail Order

Approach the table within three minutes after the guests are seated.

Greet the Guests

In a comfortable and relaxed manner, greet the guests courteously. For example, "Good evening. Welcome to Marina Landing." You may wish to introduce yourself, but you should avoid the phrase, "Hi, I'm Sam. I'll be your waiter tonight," as it has been overused.

Point Out the Specials and Wines

Show guests where the daily specials are listed on the menu. You may also want to describe any special that is unusual, such as amberjack fish.

Explain that we have a nice selection of wines by the glass or bottle, and direct them to the wine list on the table, as well as the additional wines listed in the menu. You may also want to indicate the special cocktails described on the menu.

During breakfast, explain that there is a buffet, and ask if they've ever tried the buffet. Describe the items on the buffet mentioning the hot items. Use greater detail for those guests who are unfamiliar with the buffet. Offer to walk guests through the buffet.

Take the Cocktail Order

If guests do not already have cocktails from the lounge, suggest them. You might say, for example, "What may I get you from the bar this evening? We make a very good Premium Margarita."

When taking any order, always know who ordered which item so you do not have to ask when you serve. If you cannot rely on memory, use the following procedure to number guests on a piece of paper.

Pick a place to stand at the table, and take all orders from that same spot. Number seats 1, 2, 3, etc. in a clockwise order starting from your left. If a lady is in seat #2 and a gentlemen in seat #1, you would want to take the lady's order first, even though you designate her as guest #2. (Although it is polite for gentlemen to order for their ladies, it is more common today to look at the lady for her order.) Indicate the guest number to the right of the item ordered on your pad.

If guests already have cocktails, place fresh cocktail napkins under their drinks. Check to see if refills are needed on drinks that are nearly empty. Indicate that you will be back after they've had an opportunity to look at the menu, and that you'd be happy to answer any questions about the menu.

Serve Cocktails

Serve ladies first. Whenever possible, serve from the guest's right. It is correct to serve beverages with the right hand, while carrying your tray in your left hand. Place a cocktail napkin on the guest's right, and place the drink on the napkin. Always handle glasses by the base or stem—*do not touch the rims of glasses with your hands.*

Always use a tray to carry any items to the table, including cocktails. Even if you are serving only one drink, it should be carried on a tray.

Suggest Appetizers

Now is a good time to suggest appetizers. You can sometimes get an appetizer order before taking the order for the main course. Ask if guests would like an appetizer while looking over the menu. Mention specific selections, point them out on the menu, describe them to the guests, and answer any questions the guests may have. Guests who are hungry will appreciate your thoughtfulness in getting appetizers to them promptly.

Suggest sharing appetizers, especially for lunch.

If guests are ready to order the main course at this time, take the order. Be especially sensitive to guests who have waited a long time for a table, as they may wish to order as soon as possible, even on your first trip to the table.

Take the Food Order

When guests have had a chance to look over the menu, take the order.

Know the Menu

Your menu knowledge is the most important way you can assist guests in ordering. For example, you might indicate the fresh fish selections. Know the ingredients in and preparation of each menu item, so you can intelligently describe items to the guests and answer their questions. We are known for our fresh trout, so these preparations make excellent suggestions.

Make Recommendations

If a guest needs assistance, make recommendations. Find out if the guest fancies fish or meat. For lunch, ask if the guest prefers a light meal or something more substantial. Make appropriate suggestions. For example, "The salmon is in season, and our chefs do an excellent job preparing it." You might suggest items you especially like.

Compliment the Guest's Selection

Make the guests feel comfortable with their selections, so they will be pleasantly anticipating their meal. For example, "The stuffed shrimp is an excellent choice. It's one of our most popular items."

Take the Soup and Salad Order

Be sure to ask for the guests' selection of soup or salad, naming the available soups. If the guest prefers salad, name the dressings and ask which the guest prefers.

Repeat the Order

Repeating the order to the guests avoids errors and saves time. Be sure always to ask guests how they would like their steaks and burgers prepared.

Suggest Appetizers

Suggest appetizers at this time if you have not already done so.

Suggest Wine

Suggest wine with dinner. The proper time to suggest wine is after the guest has ordered the meal, so you will know which wines to suggest to complement the food selection. For parties of four or more, you may want to suggest two bottles of wine, one with appetizers and a different wine with the entrees. (If guests do not want cocktails, you should suggest wine on the first trip to the table.) Use the wine list to help you. If guests are eating a combination of meat and fish, you might suggest both red and white wine by the glass. Be sure you can pronounce the names of the wines, describe the wines, know which wines to suggest with food items, and serve wine correctly at the table.

After you are finished taking the order, remove the menus and assure the guests that their appetizers (or soup and salad) will be served shortly. If the guests are not going to be drinking wine, remove the wine glasses as well.

Serve Bread

Be sure the bun runner arrives at the table shortly after you have taken the order. The bun runner should offer guests a selection of warm rolls and freshly baked muffins. Be sure to place butter on the table prior to the bun runner's arrival.

Serve Appetizers

The correct way of serving food is to first place the necessary silverware on the table, forks to the guest's left and knives and spoons to the guest's right. Appetizers, as well as all food, should be served to ladies, children, and elderly first. Whenever possible, food should be served from the guest's left. Try to avoid reaching over guests when serving. Food should be served with the left hand. For booths, serve people on the right with your left hand, and people on the left with your right hand.

If an appetizer is being shared, place it in the center or between guests who are sharing, and place small plates in front of each guest.

Clear Appetizers

Whenever possible, clear from the right. Remove all soiled silverware, and replace items that will be needed for later courses. Silverware should be carried to the table on a clean napkin placed on a plate. Be especially alert to replacing soiled silverware during breakfast. Sometimes guests will use a knife to eat their appetizers or salad. In these cases, the soiled knife must be cleared and replaced with a clean knife before the next course is served.

Empty cocktail glasses should be cleared promptly. They should never be left on the table until the end of the meal. Servers are to clear empty cocktail glasses during service and bussers are to clear them at the end of the meal.

Serve Soup and Salad

Place soup spoons to the right of the guest. Salad should be served on a chilled plate, and soup in a warm bowl. Be sure the soup is piping hot. Offer freshly ground pepper from the mill to guests eating salad.

Clear Soup and Salad

Clear soup and salad when guests have finished. If a guest has used the dinner knife for the salad course, remove the soiled knife and replace it with a clean one. Knives should be placed to the guest's right side with blades toward the center. Each course should be cleared completely, so be sure to remove any dressings on the side as well. Also remove any muffin wrappers or extra plates that were served earlier.

Serve Wine

It is correct to serve wine immediately before the main course. However, if guests are not having cocktails or have finished their cocktails early on, they may want to have their wine earlier in the meal. When in doubt, ask guests when they would like their wine served.

Red wines should be opened prior to serving to allow them to breathe. Explain this to guests, so they will not think you forgot to pour the wine.

The correct way to serve wine will be discussed in a separate procedure.

Serve the Main Course
Time Your Orders

Try to time your orders correctly, so the main course is ready after guests have finished their salad (or soup). If the main course is ready while guests are still having their salad, place salad plates to the left of the guest, and serve the main course, provided the guest does not object to this. If the guest wants to finish the salad and not be rushed, bring the entrees back to the kitchen. Proper timing can avoid these problems.

Serve the Food

Be sure the hot food is piping hot. Serve ladies first from the left. The entree should face the guest, and any vegetable or garnish should face the center of the table. Side dishes should be placed to the guest's left.

Explain the sauces. Offer to serve sauces to the guest. When serving sauces, do so from the guest's left. Ask if the guests need anything else. Tell them to enjoy their meal. You might indicate that you will be close by if they need anything else.

Monitor the Table

Refill wine glasses, remove empty cocktail glasses, refill water glasses, and change ashtrays. Some guests may need refills on their cocktails or they may want a soft drink with dinner. These things should be monitored throughout service.

Change ashtrays when they have one butt in them. Change them by using the capping method to prevent ashes from flying into the food.

Check Back

After guests have taken a bite or two, check back to be sure the meals are prepared the way they ordered them. Avoid the phrase, "Is everything okay?" as this is overused. "Are you enjoying your meal?" or "How are your dinners this evening?" are better phrases.

Be sensitive to any negative reaction from the guest. Sometimes a guest will be reluctant to say that something is wrong, although you will get a signal to that effect, such as a frown or a hesitation in answering your question. In this case, probe to find out if there is a problem. We want all guests to be satisfied, and *before* they eat their meal is the time to find out about and correct any problems. For example, a steak may be over- or undercooked. These problems can easily be corrected if you find out about them early in the meal.

Keep a watchful eye on the table throughout the meal.

Clear the Main Course

When guests have finished eating, clear the plates. Try to be sure each guest is truly finished before clearing the plate, and avoid bothering guests by asking them several times if they are through when in fact they are not.

Clear Thoroughly

When all guests have finished, clear the table thoroughly. Bring a tray and tray stand to the table. Have a clean, damp rag and clean butter dish on the tray. Remove sauces, side dishes, empty glasses, empty wine bottles, condiment bottles, etc. If the table needs crumbing, wipe it with a clean, damp rag, brushing crumbs into a clean butter plate held below the table rim. (Do not brush crumbs into your hand.) Water glasses, ashtray, unfinished drinks, and dessert silverware should be the only items left on the table after the main course. The table should look clean and uncluttered. (For example, if a guest did not use the dinner knife, the clean knife should be cleared after the main course, as it is not part of the dessert silverware.)

Remove Bread Plates

Be sure to remove bread plates and butter after the main course is completed. This is correct service and will improve your dessert sales. Of course, if the guest requests muffins for dessert, we are happy to accommodate him, but this should not be encouraged. The bun runner should not return to the table after the main course is completed, unless requested to by the guest.

Take the Dessert Order
Suggest Dessert

After the main course has been cleared, **bring the dessert tray to the table,** and show guests the dessert menu. Suggest specific items to them. You might also mention that we make our own gelato or that we have a selection of ice cream desserts, as well. Tell guests that we have our own bakery on the premises. If guests are full, encourage sharing.

Suggest Specialty Coffees

Also suggest the specialty coffees. For example, "Would you like Irish coffee or regular?" will sell many Irish coffees and offer guests something unusual that they had not thought of themselves. Also suggest after-dinner drinks, such as cognacs and liqueurs.

Serve Desserts and Coffee

Desserts and coffee, as well as any other items, should always be brought to the table on a tray. Place the necessary silverware on the table. Whenever possible, serve desserts from the left, using the left hand. Cakes and pies should be placed with the point of the wedge facing the guest. If guests are sharing, bring additional silverware and plates, as necessary. Silverware should be placed on the table, not on the dessert plates.

Serve coffee from the right, when possible. Coffee cups should be placed to the guest's right, with handles at the 4 o'clock position. The correct way to pour coffee is to first place the cup on the table, then pour the coffee from the guest's right.

Clear Desserts

Dessert dishes and silverware should be cleared when guests have finished; however, coffee cups should remain on the table until guests have left. Refill coffee and tea as necessary.

If guests are lingering over coffee, they might enjoy an after-dinner drink. They might not think of it on their own, but would appreciate a suggestion from you. Suggest a fine cognac, such as Courvoisier, for men, or a liqueur, such as Sambucca or Amaretto, for women.

Present the Check

During lunch, be sure the check is presented promptly after guests have finished their meal. For dinner, it is correct to wait for guests to ask for the check, but many guests do not realize this. After dessert is completed and cleared, and you are sure that there is nothing else the guest wants, present the check. Place it face-down on a tip tray to the right of the host. If it is not clear who the host is, place the check between the men at the table, or in the center of the table. Thank the guests.

Close Service

When you bring guests their change or credit card voucher for signing, thank them warmly for their visit. When a credit card is used for payment, make a note of the guest's name and use it. For example, say, "Thank you, Mr. Smith." This adds a personal touch.

Whenever possible, assist guests with their coats, and tell them to come and see us again.

Prepare Table for Next Guests
Bring Tray to Table and Clear Table

After guests have left, the busperson (or waitperson, if the busser is busy) should bring a tray to the table. This is necessary in order to do a proper job of clearing the table and to do it all in one trip. It saves time to clear with a tray. The tray should not be placed all over the table, but just set at one corner. Everything should be placed on the tray. Glasses should be handled by the base. Do not put your hands inside glasses—this is still unsanitary even if the guests are no longer sitting at the table. Silverware and other items should not be placed inside the glasses, as this is unsightly. The table should be wiped with a clean, white rag. Gather crumbs to the corner where your tray is, then lift the tray and sweep the crumbs into it.

Another rag should be used to wipe the crumbs off the seats before leaving the table. Separate rags should always be used for tables and chairs. Be sure tables and chairs are clean and free from crumbs. Push chairs in close to the table.

Be aware that guests at other tables are watching you.

Reset

Reset the table for the next party.

General Considerations
Serving Alcoholic Beverages

We encourage you to suggest alcohol to guests, but not if they are minors or if they show signs of being intoxicated. You should all know that it is unlawful to serve alcohol to these two groups, and we make every effort to abide by the law.

Serving Food and Beverages

The correct way of serving is to serve food from the left using the left hand, and to serve beverages from the right, using the right hand. Do this whenever possible. For booths, serve people on your left with your right hand, and people on the right with your left hand. Using the hand opposite the guest is more graceful and avoids bumping the guest in the face with your elbow.

Use a Tray

Always use a tray for carrying things to and from the table. For example, cocktails, even just one glass, should always be carried on a tray. Silverware brought to the table should always be carried on a tray, as well.

Handle Wares in a Sanitary Manner

Silverware, glassware, dishes, etc., should not be touched on the eating surfaces. Keep thumbs out of plates, handle glasses by the base or stem, and touch silverware on the handles only.

Wipe Silverware and Check Glasses

Silverware should be wiped before it is rolled for table setups. Glassware should be inspected for smudges, fingerprints, and lipstick marks. If the staff gets into the habit of handling glasses by the stems and bases, there should not be fingerprints on the glasses.

Be Sensitive to Guests' Wishes

If the guests indicates that they want a certain kind of service, be receptive to their wishes. For example, sometimes guests will be deeply involved in a serious conversation and would like minimal contact with the server. They will give signals to the server that they do not want to be disturbed, such as by barely looking at the server and discouraging conversation. In cases like this, keep conversation to a minimum.

Be Sensitive To Guests' Special Needs

Pay special attention to children, and do what you can to keep them occupied. Elderly and handicapped people may need additional assistance.

Resolve Complaints so the Guest Is Happy

It is our policy to be sure that every guest leaves satisfied. If there is a complaint, apologize and take corrective action. Notify the manager if necessary. Studies have shown that unhappy guests will tell up to ten people about their bad experience at a restaurant. We all need to do our part to be sure that guests enjoy their dining experience and recommend us to their acquaintances.

Use Good Judgment

The rules of service are general guidelines, but they need to be applied by you in specific circumstances. Sometimes they will not apply. For example, if a party is in a hurry and some want to eat dessert while the others are finishing their meal, by all means comply with their wishes even though it is not correct to serve desserts until all have finished the main course. Always use your judgment in serving your guests.

Stay on Your Station and Be Attentive

Socializing with co-workers should not be done during service. When you are on duty, this is business and we're in the business of pleasing our guests. In order to be attentive to the needs of the guests, you have to stay on your station watching your tables.

Appendix B: Service Situations*

Read the following situations and ask yourself: What did the waiter do right and what did he do wrong? List the things that were done incorrectly at the bottom and indicate how you would have done them better.

Service Situation #1
The Start of the Meal

The hostess brings four guests to the table. The guests seat themselves. The waiter comes over and places bread and menus on the table and says, "I'll be right with you." One guest asks a busboy for an ashtray and the busboy brings it. The waiter comes back in a while and asks, "Okay, ready to order?" The guests order dinner and drinks. Since only two drinks were ordered, the waiter places them in one hand and carries them to the table. Next, the waiter brings the appetizers. He checks with the guests to be sure he is serving the correct dishes to the people who ordered them. He walks away as the guests put their cigarettes out and begin to eat.

---

*Courtesy of Hospitality Industry Training, Inc.

How could the waiter have improved his service?

_____

_____

_____

Service Situation #2
Serving the Main Course

The busboy clears each appetizer as it is finished. Where knives were used with the appetizer, the busboy is careful to place the knives back on the table for use with the main course. He takes the soiled ashtray off the table, dumps the ashes into one of the dirty dishes he is carrying, and puts the ashtray back on the table. (He turns his back so guests won't see him dumping the ashes.)

The waiter serves the main course and tells the guests to enjoy their meal. One of the guests ask about wine, so the waiter brings the wine list to the table. Wine is ordered, and the waiter promptly serves it.

After the guests finish eating, the busboy, standing in one place, clears off all of the plates. He leaves the bread, in case the guests want to continue picking at it. He removes the empty wine and water glasses from the table. He leaves the steak sauce and ketchup on the table for the next customers who will be eating there.

How could the waiter and busboy have improved their service?

_____

_____

_____

_____

_____

_____

_____

Service Situation #3
Serving Dessert and Closing Service

After the busboy has cleared the table, the waiter approaches and asks, "Can I get you anything else?" Two of the guests point to a neighboring table, and say they would like to have the same dessert their neighbors are having. All four guests order coffee. The waiter brings the coffee before the dessert. For safety reasons, he fills the coffee cups on his cocktail tray, then places them on the table. Next he serves the desserts. He then asks the busboy to bring forks to the table for the desserts. While the guests are having their dessert, the waiter puts the check on the table, face-up, by the host. The guests request more coffee and the waiter refills the cups.

When the guests finally leave, the waiter and busboy clear and reset the table. They remove remaining glasses by placing their hands in them, so they can carry away more at one time. They change the tablecloth by placing the salt and pepper and condiments on the chair and removing the soiled cloth. They cover the blue foam pad under the table cloth with a clean cloth. Then they place the condiments back on the table. One of them brings clean silverware over, carrying it in his hand. and sets the table. They push the chairs in close to the table and get ready for the next guests.

How could the waiter and busboy have improved their service?

_____
_____
_____
_____
_____
_____
_____

Service Situation #4
Serving Wine

Guests have ordered a bottle of red wine. They are drinking cocktails and eating salad. The waitress brings the wine to the table. While holding the wine in one hand, she begins to open the bottle with her corkscrew in the other hand. She first removes the lead cap and places it on the table. Next she twists the corkscrew into the cork and pulls the cork out. She places the cork in her pocket. Next, she pours a little wine for the host to taste. He tastes it and approves of the wine. Then, she fills the wine glasses to the top with wine and leaves the bottle on the table. She smiles and walks away.

The waitress notices that another of her parties needs replenishing of their wine. This party is drinking a white wine. She removes the wine from the ice bucket and refills the glasses. The bottle is now empty, so she turns the bottle upside down in the ice bucket and walks away.

How could the waitress have improved her wine service?

_____

_____

_____

_____

_____

_____

_____

Appendix C: Suggestive Selling Techniques*

The Professional Server: How to Increase Sales and Tips

Refer to the video program for an explanation of each point.

Prerequisites to Selling

Be convinced that selling benefits you and the guest.

Know your products.

Be enthusiastic about your products.

Look attractive.

The Techniques

1. Upgrade the guest's choice.

2. Be specific.

---

*From "The Professional Server: How to Increase Sales and Tips," Training Guide accompanying videotape. Sponsor: *Restaurant Business* magazine.

3. Assume the guest wants to buy.

4. Describe items, giving the facts and a positive evaluation.

5. Use props.

6. Find out what the guest wants.

7. Use good timing.

8. Suggest sharing.

9. Offer a taste (with management's permission).

10. Compliment the guest's choice.

Points to Remember

Give good service in general. Selling is only part of taking care of the guest.

Do not suggest or serve alcohol to minors to to intoxicated individuals. Follow your state's liquor code and your restaurant's policies regarding the responsible service of alcohol.

Appendix D: Exercise on Suggestive Selling Techniques*

1. What kind of cocktail might you suggest on a warm summer day, and how would you describe it? _____
   _____

   What cocktail might you suggest on a cold winter day, and how would you describe it? _____
   _____

2. Name 2 appetizers which you especially like:
   (A) _____ (B) _____
   How would you describe them to your guests?
   (A) _____
   (B) _____

3. Which wine would you recommend with fish, and how would you describe it? _____
   _____

   Which wine would you recommend with red meat, and how would you describe it? _____
   _____
   _____

_____

*Courtesy of Hospitality Industry Training, Inc.

4. Describe 2 of your favorite desserts which are served in your restaurant:

_____

_____

_____

_____

What dessert(s) would you recommend to someone who is dieting? ____

_____

5. What after-dinner liqueurs might you suggest to women? _____

_____

_____

What after-dinner drinks might you suggest to men? _____

_____

_____

6. What other items do you, or would you like to, suggest? _____

_____

_____

_____

Appendix E: Sample Questions from a Menu Quiz*

For multiple-choice questions, circle the one correct letter.

1. Name the type of snails used in escargot. _____

2. (T or F) Snails are in ocean waters and delivered to us alive in their shells. _____

3. Which is a true statement about the escargot butter?
   - (A) it contains garlic
   - (B) it contains Pernod
   - (C) it contains Sauterne
   - (D) A & B only
   - (E) A & C only
   - (F) A, B, & C

4. (T or F) The smoked trout is fresh, never frozen. _____

5. (T or F) The smoked trout is made with fresh trout from our Simms Landing trout tank. _____

_____

*Courtesy of Simms Landing.

6. The trout is smoked using a:
   (A) cold smoking process
   (B) hot smoking process

7. Give the brand name of crackers served with the smoked trout.

_____

8. The mustard-dill sauce served with the smoked trout contains:
   (A) Pernod
   (B) Sauterne
   (C) soy sauce
   (D) honey
   (E) C & D only
   (F) all of the above

9. Name the *style* of mustard used in the mustard-dill sauce.

_____

10. Phylo dough is used in which famous Greek product?
    (A) moussaka
    (B) baklava
    (C) stuffed grape leaves
    (D) all of the above

Appendix F: Quiz on Wines by the Glass*

All questions pertain to the wines by the glass offered by your restaurant. Your answers should only pertain to this wine list.

1-5. Name the 5 white wines served by the glass.

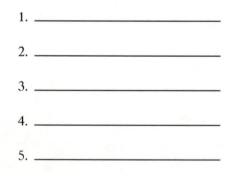

     1. _____

     2. _____

     3. _____

     4. _____

     5. _____

6. Give the brand name of our house Chardonnay. _____

7. (Answer true or false) One Chardonnay on our wine list is from Germany while the other is from California. _____

---

*Courtesy of Marina Landing.

8. (Answer true or false) The Chardonnays are dry white wines.

_____

9. Which Chardonnay is the heavier, weightier, and more substantial one?

_____

10. Which Chardonnay is the lighter, citrus-style one?   _____

11. Which Chardonnay has more oak flavor?   _____

12. From what grape is the Fume Blanc made?   _____

13. Which white wine is perfect with shellfish and seafood? _____

14. (Answer true or false) Fume Blanc is a sweet white wine.

_____

15. Excluding the dessert wine, which white wine is the sweetest one on the list?   _____

16. Which white wine is a good beginner's wine and does not need an acquired taste to be enjoyed?   _____

17. Which white wine would be described as a medium-dry white wine?

_____

18. Which of the white wines contains 10% alcohol, lower than most other California wines?   _____

19-20. What 2 questions are most important to ask the guest to determine his or her taste in wine so that you can make an appropriate wine recommendation?

19. _____

20. _____

21-22. Name the 2 blush wines offered by the glass, brand name included:

21. _____

22. _____

23. (Answer true or false) Blush wines are made from red wine grapes.

_____

24. (Answer true or false) Blush wines taste more like red wines than whites.

_____

25. Which blush wine is more substantial and drier tasting? _____

26. What grape is used to make the blush wine described in question 25?

_____

27-29. Name the 3 red wines sold by the glass:

27. _____

28. _____

29. _____

30. (Answer true or false) The 3 red wines on the list are all made from the same grape.   _____

31. (Answer true or false) French Bordeaux wines are made from the Zinfandel grape.   _____

32. (Answer true or false) Red wines are more popular than whites.

_____

33. The puckery feeling that red wines leave in the mouth is due to what substance in the red wine?   _____

34. Which red wine is the lightest and fruitiest?   _____

35. Which red wine is a little drier than the others?

_____

36. (Answer true or false) Red wines normally go well with lighter entrees such as chicken and seafood.   _____

37. (Answer true or false) Sparkling wines are appropriate with appetizers, entrees, or desserts.   _____

38. Name the Spanish sparkling wine on the list.   _____

39. Name the French sparkling wine on the list. _____

40. Which sparkling wine is very dry? _____

41. Which sparkling wine is fruitier? _____

42. Name the California dessert wine on the list. _____

43. From what grape is the California dessert wine made? _____

44. Name the sherry on the list. _____

45. Name the port wine on the list. _____

46. (Answer true or false) All sherries are sweet wines. _____

47. (Choose one) Which of the following are true statements about sherries and ports:
       a. They are fortified wines.
       b. They are fortified with brandy or another spirit.
       c. They contain up to 18-20% alcohol.
       d. All of the above.

48. (Answer true or false) Red wines, sherries, and ports are drunk more during the summertime. _____

49. What would you suggest if someone ordered trout for dinner and liked sweet wine?

_____

_____

50. What wine would you suggest with a steak dinner?

_____

*Appendix G: Self-analysis Exercise for Servers**

Read over the "Rules and Sequence of Service," and evaluate your service. Identify your strong points and also those areas where improvement is possible. Also decide what you will do to improve. Remember that a 2% increase in your average tip percentage could mean a difference of a few thousand dollars in your income for the year.

Rating Scale: A = Excellent—needs no improvement
              B = Good—but can still improve
              C = Fair—can improve a lot

Appearance (A-B-C)

My strong points are _____

_____

I can improve in the following ways _____

_____

What I will do to improve _____

_____

---

*Courtesy of Simms Landing.

Attitude/Friendliness/
Hospitality Toward Guests (A-B-C)

My strong points are _____

_____

I can improve in the following ways _____

_____

What I will do to improve _____

_____

Technical Skills (A-B-C)

My strong points are _____

_____

I can improve in the following ways _____

_____

What I will do to improve _____

_____

Suggestive Selling Skills (A-B-C)

My strong points are _____

_____

I can improve in the following ways _____

_____

What I will do to improve _____

_____

Overall Rating of Myself as a Server (A-B-C)

*Appendix H: Checklist for Service Role-play**

Instructions to the Servers

- The purpose of this exercise is for you to practice all the rules of good service and suggestive selling skills.

- Look over this form and the Rules of Service prior to beginning the role-play.

- Use menus, trays, glasses, utensils, plates, and other equipment.

- Do not use food. Only water and wine glasses filled with water will be served, eveything else is mock.

Instructions to the Guests

- The purpose of this exercise is to experience dining at Marina as a guest and to evaluate the service you receive.

- Ask the server questions about menu items and wines.

---

*Courtesy of Marina Landing.

• Give the server every opportunity to suggest side items to you, such as cocktails, appetizers, wine, desserts, and after-dinner drinks.

• Order cocktails, appetizers, wine, dessert, and after-dinner drinks.

• Read the checklist carefully and, during the meal, make notes of the server's service and suggestive selling skills.

	YES	NO
1. Was the table set properly?	_____	_____
2. Was the server neat, clean, well groomed?	_____	_____

3. How was the server's greeting? (circle one)
    cool   polite, but reserved
    very warm and friendly		

4. Were the specials and wines pointed out?	_____	_____
5. Was the water poured properly?	_____	_____
6. Were cocktails suggested?	_____	_____
7. Did the server show good knowledge of drinks?	_____	_____
8. Were the drinks served on a tray, from the right side and with the right hand?	_____	_____
9. Was the dinner order taken properly?	_____	_____
10. Did the server show good knowledge of the menu?	_____	_____
11. Was an appropriate wine suggested?	_____	_____
12. Did the server show good knowledge of wines?	_____	_____
13. Were appetizers suggested?	_____	_____
14. Did the server mention specific appetizers and describe them in accurate and appealing terms?	_____	_____
15. Were the appetizers served correctly—ladies first, with left hand from the left side, without asking who gets what?	_____	_____

16. Did the server bus the table properly after appetizers?   _____   _____

17. Were salads and soups served correctly?   _____   _____

18. Was freshly ground pepper offered for salad?   _____   _____

19. Was the table bussed properly after salads and were utensils replaced?   _____   _____

20. Did the server carry everything to the table on a tray?   _____   _____

21. Was the wine served properly? (Show host label, open properly, present cork to host, pour taster, etc.)   _____   _____

22. Was the main course served properly? (From left with left hand, ladies first, without asking who gets what, sauces explained, side dishes to left, etc.)   _____   _____

23. Did the server check back to see if all was satisfactory?   _____   _____

24. Were ashtrays changed when they had one butt and changed by the capping method?   _____   _____

25. Was the table cleared thoroughly after the entree course?   _____   _____

26. Were desserts suggested?   _____   _____

27. Did the server show good knowledge of desserts?   _____   _____

28. Were specific suggestions made and were items described in appealing and descriptive terms?   _____   _____

29. Were specific after-dinner drinks suggested?   _____   _____

30. Were coffee and dessert served properly? (Dessert from left, coffee from right)   _____   _____

31. Was the table cleared properly after dessert? _____ _____

32. Did the server close sevice properly? _____ _____

Rate the Server A, B, C, OR F:

Enthusiasm and attitude _____
Service skills _____
Suggestive selling skills _____
Appearance _____
Posture and manner _____
OVERALL _____

The server's strong points are: _____
_____
_____

Recommendations for improvement are: _____
_____
_____

Additional comments: _____
_____
_____
_____

Index